Summer
Smoothies

Summer Smoothies

*Over 130
Cool and Refreshing
Recipes*

Donna Pliner Rodnitzky

PRIMA PUBLISHING

Published by Prima Publishing, Roseville, California. Member of
the Crown Publishing Group, a division of Random House, Inc.

PRIMA PUBLISHING and colophon are trademarks of Random
House, Inc., registered with the United States Patent and Trade-
mark Office.

A per serving nutritional breakdown is provided for each recipe.
If a range is given for an ingredient amount, the breakdown is
based on the smaller number. If a range is given for servings, the
breakdown is also based on the smaller number. If a choice of ingredients is given in an ingredient listing, the breakdown is calcu-
lated using the first choice. Nutritional content may vary
depending on the specific brands or types of ingredients used.
"Optional" ingredients or those for which no specific amount is
stated are not included in the breakdown. Nutritional figures are
rounded to the nearest whole number.

Library of Congress Cataloging-in-Publication data on file

ISBN: 0-7615-3732-5

02 03 04 05 06 HH 10 9 8 7 6 5 4 3 2 1
Printed in the United States of America

First Edition

Visit us online at www.primapublishing.com

To my husband, Bob, my companion for over thirty years. You have encouraged me in all my endeavors and have been a rich source of novel ideas and constructive critiques. And to my children, David, Adam, and Laura, whose accomplishments and deeds continue to be a source of tremendous pride and inspiration for me.

Contents

Acknowledgments

I would like to thank my acquisitions editor, Denise Sternad, for encouraging me to write another smoothie cookbook. It is a great challenge, and privilege, to once again have the opportunity to meet the high standards of Prima Publishing. I would also like to thank my project editor, Michelle McCormack, who has been a pleasure to work with these past years. I am always confident that she will give her utmost attention to every detail and provide insightful and invaluable suggestions. Thanks to Monica Thomas, cover designer, and the entire staff at Prima Publishing for their excellent professionalism in bringing this book to publication.

Introduction

Smoothies are one of the most appealing trends of our time. They have become the "in" drink for health-conscious individuals seeking novel and nutritious ways to enrich their diets without adding too many calories or unnecessary fat. At the same time, many of us enjoy smoothies for the sheer pleasure of indulging in a refreshing taste sensation that is delicious and filling.

Although the popularity of smoothies is due largely to their nutritional benefits and great taste, another plus is their ease of preparation. For many of us with busy lifestyles, it's difficult to find the time to prepare healthful foods for our daily diets, yet a smoothie creation, made of the simplest ingredients, can be prepared in minutes. Even though the most elementary smoothies are made with a simple combination of fruit and fruit juice, with the availability of such a great variety of seasonal fruits and juices, these wonders in a glass can be amazingly rewarding. Beyond the basics, a dairy product, such as milk or yogurt, can be substituted for the juice or included as an additional ingredient. Best of all, these ingredients can all be blended into an infinite number of delectable combinations, limited only by your imagination.

Whether you choose to drink a smoothie for its nutritional qualities or simply because it's delicious, you can't help benefiting from its inherently healthful ingredients. Smoothies are chock full of vitamins from the fruit, and their dairy ingredients are a rich source of calcium. These delightful drinks can also be supplemented with a wide variety of healthful additives or soybean products that quickly transform them into an even more nutritionally balanced and wholesome treat.

Summer Smoothies appropriately begins with a chapter titled "Health Benefits of Smoothies." Here, you'll learn why smoothies are so good for you and find suggestions on how to maximize their nutritional value. In chapter 2, "About Fruit—Noteworthy Ingredients: How to Select, Prepare, and Store Fresh Fruit," you'll discover the secrets of selecting and preparing the best fruits for the ultimate smoothie. Finally, if you're unfamiliar with the equipment needed to make a smoothie, chapter 3, "Getting Started—Making a Summer Smoothie: Equipment and Techniques," will prove to be very useful to you. This chapter concentrates on the essential tools you need to transform your kitchen into Smoothie Central. You'll also discover a host of helpful techniques that will enable you to elevate every blender masterpiece you prepare to the absolute pinnacle of smoothiedom.

Chapter 4, the first recipe chapter, "Simple Pleasures: All-Time Summer Favorites," will appeal to all smoothie devotees. You'll learn that to make a basic smoothie, you simply combine your favorite richly flavored fruit and fruit juice in a blender and rev it up. Your reward will be a scrumptious smoothie. Some of my favorites are

Macho, Macho Mango, a pleasantly sweet blend of mangoes, bananas, strawberries, and pineapple juice, and *California Whirls,* made with a tantalizing combination of strawberries, pineapple, banana, and apricot nectar.

Chapter 5, "M*ooo*town Smoothies: Dare-E to Be Different," presents delectable smoothies made with dairy products, such as milk and yogurt. You'll discover that with the addition of dairy ingredients, you can endow smoothies with a creamier consistency and richer flavor. In most of the recipes, I suggest using lowfat dairy products to keep the fat content to a minimum. However, depending on your diet, whole dairy products can be substituted, or lowfat ones can be replaced with fat-free ingredients and vice versa. Any of these substitutions will not appreciably change the taste or consistency of the smoothie. So fall in love with a glassful of *Cantaloupe? Need a Ladder!,* made with a luscious blend of cantaloupe, banana, orange juice, and vanilla yogurt, or savor a serving of *Supermango,* a dairy delight made with mango, banana, peach nectar, and vanilla frozen yogurt.

Chapter 6, "Smoothie Power: Fit and Trim, Filled to the Rim," contains many recipes made with soybean products as well as several that feature the addition of other health-enhancing supplements. Although smoothies usually provide a healthy dose of vitamins and calcium derived from their fruit and dairy ingredients, they do not ordinarily qualify as a nutritionally complete meal replacement but typically are enjoyed as a nutritious snack or a supplement to a meal. However, when you would like to transform a smoothie into an instant meal, this chapter will guide you in the use of nutritional additives, breakfast powders, or protein supplements to achieve this goal. Just as their mealworthiness can be improved, you'll learn how the health benefits of smoothies can be enhanced as well by the simple addition of supplements, such as herbs or extracts. What's more, these additives and supplements can be added without appreciably changing the smoothie's taste or texture. If you're looking for a delicious way to increase the fiber in your diet, try starting the morning with a glass of *How Wheat It Is,* made with orange juice, soy milk, cherries, banana, blackberries, tofu, and wheat germ; or, when you're in need of a quick energy boost, consider mixing up a batch of *Triathlon Turbo,* a high-energy blend that packs a punch derived from soy milk, orange juice, blueberries, raspberries, banana, protein powder, wheat germ, and bee pollen.

While smoothies are usually enjoyed as a refreshing break during a busy day, there may be some occasions when you have the urge to splurge on something that is more outrageously decadent. For such mildly sinful indulgences, you need look no further than chapter 7, "Dazzling Dessert Smoothies: Decadence in a Glass." When a smoothie is made with rich ingredients, such as ice cream, hot fudge sauce, and other temptingly caloric additions that are not usually associated with these healthful drinks, the resulting decadent delight can share center stage with any chocolate mousse or flaming dessert. While these smoothies are meant to be an occasional indulgence, keep in mind that there is no prohibition against substituting lowfat yogurt or ice cream for traditional ice cream. So, if you adore coffee and ice cream, you're certain to be delighted with a serving of *Daddy Starbucks*, a luscious combination of coffee, hot fudge sauce, banana, and caramel ice cream; or, if you prefer the tastes of the tropics, try sampling *Good Golly, Miss Maui*, a heavenly Hawaiian combination of pineapple and banana with coconut gelato.

Chapter 8, "Cocktail Hour: Perfect Party Smoothies," presents recipes for smoothies meant to be served on those special occasions when a celebration is in order. Laced with your favorite spirits, these smoothies acquire a delectable taste that lingers long after the last straw full, and, when accented with an edible garnish, they can grace an elegant dessert plate or become the grand finale of a candlelight dinner. The next time you're looking for a special smoothie that is certain to impress your friends, consider offering them a balloon glass filled with *Brandy Alexander*, a creamy blend of brandy, crème de cacao, banana, and ice cream. Don't forget to garnish it by inserting a *Spritz Cookie* or two *Cinnamon-Coated Fusilli* (both found in chapter 9) standing upright in the center of the smoothie.

Finally, chapter 9, "Glorious Garnishes: A Touch of Class," contains several recipes for garnishes that will enable you to transform any of your favorite smoothie creations into a visually striking presentation. While some of these adornments are more elaborate, I have also included others that are quick and easy to prepare and can be made ahead of time. For your most discerning guests, you'll want to try a *Cinnamon-Coated Tortilla Triangle,* an attractive and flavorful way to accent an indulgent smoothie. On the lighter side, consider adding an *Apple Chip* or *Pineapple Chip,* a simple touch that will tastefully decorate the most basic smoothie.

Once considered only a simple combination of fruit and fruit juice, smoothies have definitely grown up and now consist of a dazzling array of appealing and sometimes exotic combinations. So what are you waiting for? Rev up the blender and get ready for some excitement in a glass.

C H A P T E R

I

Health Benefits of Smoothies

With today's trend toward a healthier lifestyle, it comes as no surprise that smoothies are so popular. Whether these delectable concoctions are made with a simple combination of fruit and fruit juice, mixed with a creamy dairy product, or supplemented with a variety of health-enhancing boosters, the end result is always a nutritionally enriched drink with major health benefits.

One of the major reasons smoothies are so good for you is that they are made with fresh fruit. For many years, health authorities have encouraged us to enrich our diets by including two to three servings of fruit each day. Even with a hectic lifestyle, this lofty goal can easily be achieved simply by including a smoothie or two in our daily diet, and the health benefits can be substantial. Because fruits contain a bounty of antioxidants, complying with this recommendation reduces the risk of a wide variety of serious ailments, such as cancer, arthritis, and heart disease. What's more, these nutrient-packed powerhouses are also a rich source of fiber and minerals.

While fruits make up the largest portion of a smoothie, there are a wide variety of other ingredients that can be included to gain an additional healthful boost. Dairy products, such as milk and yogurt, can be added to provide additional calcium and protein. For those who are lactose intolerant, a product such as Rice Dream, a delicious nondairy beverage possessing the same calcium and protein value as milk, can be combined with traditional smoothie ingredients to enhance their nutritional value. Incorporating high-protein ingredients such as soy milk, soy yogurt, or tofu into a smoothie provides the opportunity to benefit from their health-enhancing properties while at the same time enjoying their unique flavors. An added benefit is that soybean products such as these are rich in calcium, iron, zinc, and fiber and are cholesterol-free, lowfat, low-sodium, and low-calorie. The addition of herbs and extracts is still another way to heighten a smoothie's health-enhancing potential. Finally, simply by including nutritional additives, such as breakfast powders or protein supplements, a smoothie can quickly be elevated to whole-meal status.

Clearly, smoothies, one of the most naturally healthful menu items, can be made still more beneficial to you with a touch or a teaspoon of the right additive. The following brief descriptions will help you better understand and effectively use these health-enhancing ingredients and wellness-promoting boosters.

- **Soy Milk and Soy Yogurt**
  Soy milk is a rich, naturally sweet beverage made from soybeans that have been finely ground and strained. Soy yogurt is made from soy milk. These products are high in protein, B vitamins, and iron. They also are low in saturated fat and packed with fiber. A diet that is low in saturated fats and rich with soy foods is believed to lower LDL ("bad") cholesterol levels. Soy milk is packaged in aseptic nonrefrigerated containers or in ordinary quart- and gallon-size milk containers found in the dairy case of most supermarkets. Soy yogurt is packaged the same way as other yogurt products and also can be found in the dairy case.

- **Silken Tofu**
  Silken tofu, with its creamy, custardlike texture, can be found in both soft and firm varieties. The former is much softer in consistency than ordinary firm tofu, making it an ideal ingredient to add to a smoothie. Silken tofu can be found in the produce section of most supermarkets as well as in the dairy or deli section. It's sold in water-filled tubs, vacuum-packed containers, or aseptic brick packages. Because it's ultrapasteurized, it has a long shelf life, but once opened, it should be refrigerated and used within three to four days.

- **Rice Dream**
  Rice Dream is a dairy-free alternative to milk that has just as much calcium and vitamins A and D. It's made from certified organic or premium California brown rice.

- **Bee Pollen**
  This natural substance is rich in ordinary and essential amino acids, the building blocks of protein. Moreover, it contains 28 minerals, most of the known vitamins, 11 enzymes, and 14 fatty acids. All these nutrients, in just the right proportions, support the body's own healing and rejuvenation mechanisms and increase energy, stamina, and endurance.

- **Brewer's Yeast**
  Brewer's yeast, sometimes called nutritional yeast, is different from baker's yeast in that its live yeast cells have been destroyed, leaving only their nutrients behind. This single-cell organism is an excellent source of vegetarian protein and is rich in major B vitamins. It also contains 16 amino acids, 14 minerals, and iron. Because Brewer's yeast is such a rich source of B vitamins, it's believed to help relieve stress, depression, irritability, and fatigue.

- **Ginkgo Biloba**
  This extract comes from the fan-shaped leaf of the ornamental ginkgo tree, a species that is reputed to be almost 200 million years old. The leaves are divided into two lobes, which accounts for the term "biloba." Ginkgo biloba will not stop the aging process, but it's thought to increase blood flow to the brain,

thereby enhancing several of the brain's functions and possibly improving some of the symptoms of Alzheimer's disease, such as memory loss.

- **Ginseng**
  Another herb, ginseng is considered by many to be one of the best supplemental and restorative agents that nature provides. Among its attributes, it's reputed to be capable of increasing mental alertness, restoring vitality, relieving stress, and enhancing immunity.

- **Flaxseed Oil**
  Flaxseed oil is rich in alpha-linolenic acid (ALA), an essential fatty acid used as a source of energy. ALA is a member of a healthful family of fats called omega-3 fatty acids. On the other hand, oils derived from corn, safflower, sesame, cottonseed, and sunflower are rich in less healthful omega-6 fatty acids. It's important to keep a balance of omega-3 and omega-6 fatty acids in the diet to prevent health problems. Because American diets tend to be high in omega-6 fatty acids and low in omega-3 fatty acids, adding an omega-3 supplement, such as flaxseed oil, to a diet helps balance the two fatty acids.

- **Spirulina**
  This bluegreen algae (single-celled plant) is named for its spiral shape. It's a tiny aquatic plant that contains easy-to-digest, all-vegetable protein, essential vitamins, iron, phytonutrients such as beta-carotene, as well as vitamins B12 and B complex. Spirulina gets its rich

green color from its rainbow of pigments, including chlorophyll (green), carotenoids (orange), and phycocyanin (blue), all of which harvest the sun's energy.

- **Wheat Germ**
Wheat germ is the germ, or "heart," of the wheat kernel. It has a wonderful nutty flavor and is packed with nutrition. Not only is it rich in insoluble fiber, but two tablespoons will provide 10% of the recommended daily requirement of folate, zinc, and magnesium and 15% of the recommended daily allowance for vitamin E and thiamine.

- **Oat and Wheat Bran**
Fiber is an important dietary constituent found in plant foods, such as vegetables, fruits, and grains. Bran, the outer part of grains, is richly endowed with fiber. Wheat bran has a higher concentration of fiber than oat bran. Dietary fiber is divided into two categories: soluble fiber found in such foods as oat bran, oatmeal, strawberries, and beans, and insoluble fiber found in foods such as wheat bran, cauliflower, cabbage, and carrots. The American Heart Association suggests eating a diet that is low in saturated fat and cholesterol but rich in both soluble and insoluble fiber. Each form of fiber has specific health benefits. Soluble fiber in the diet helps lower blood cholesterol, while insoluble fiber plays an important role in maintaining normal bowel functions.

- **Protein Powders**
  Most often, soy-based protein powders pro-vide a natural source of amino acids, vitamins, minerals, fiber, and iron.

- **Green Tea**
  Green tea contains a chemical called polyphe-nol, which is a potent antioxidant. Among the many health-enhancing qualities that have been attributed to green tea, it's reputed by some to protect against esophageal cancer, control high blood pressure, lower blood-sugar levels, and reduce cholesterol levels.

If instant refreshment packed with nutrients is what you're craving, you need look no further than your own kitchen countertop. Simply add one or more power boosters, protein powders, or soybean products to your next smoothie, and you can enjoy an energy-packed glassful that is as nutritious as it is delicious. Here's to your health!

CHAPTER 2

About Fruit–Noteworthy Ingredients

How to Select, Prepare, and Store Fresh Fruit

Fruit makes up the majority of a smoothie, so being well informed about the wide variety of options available can be very helpful in your mission to create the perfect smoothie. This chapter was designed to acquaint you with these delectable bundles of flavor and to guide you in choosing, storing, and preparing them. To begin with, it's important to realize that choosing fruit that is "smoothie ready" can be very deceptive, especially if your choice is based on appearance alone. At first glance, a peach may look ripe simply because of its rich color; however, there are a number of other less obvious attributes that are equally important. You should attempt to determine whether the fruit has a fresh aroma, how heavy or dense it is, and whether it's firm yet resilient to the touch. These are all characteristics that are often more important than the fruit's color. The good news is that once you become a fruit maven, you'll find that it's actually quite easy to determine whether fruit is ripe.

I'm certain that as you become more familiar with the fabulous array of fruit available, you'll delight, more than ever, in the excitement of making deliciously refreshing and satisfying smoothies. Whether you use the recipes found in this book or those that you're inspired to create yourself, this is going to be one of the most flavorful adventures of your life.

As you navigate the aisles of your favorite farmer's market or produce department, I hope you find the following information useful in your quest for the best nature has to offer.

APPLE

Apples are believed to have originated in Central Asia and the Caucasus, but they have been cultivated since prehistoric times. They were brought to the United States at the beginning of the seventeenth century and later to Africa and Australia. Today, there are over 100 varieties of apples commercially grown in the United States.

Apples, whether red, green, or yellow, all have a firm, crisp flesh. They are a rich source of fiber. Some apples have a sweet flavor with a hint of tartness, while others are less sweet and more tart. Most apples are delicious when made into a smoothie, but your flavor preference will determine the best variety for you.

Selection

When choosing an apple, look for one that is firm and crisp with a smooth and tight skin. Most important, the apple should have a sweet-smelling aroma. Avoid any apple that has a bruised or blemished skin. Another consideration when choosing apples is to buy the organic variety whenever possible. Most nonorganic apples are heavily sprayed with pesticides and later waxed to preserve and keep them looking fresh. Because organic apples have not been subjected to this treatment, you might find a worm in some organic apples. These unwelcome visitors can be removed when the apple is cut, thereby removing any health or aesthetic concerns. Wash in cool water and dry all apples well, whether organic or not. Apples can be stored in the crisper bin of the refrigerator for up to 6 weeks if they are kept separate from other fruits and vegetables.

APRICOT

The apricot is a round or oblong fruit measuring about two inches in diameter with skin and flesh that are golden orange in color. It's a very sweet and juicy fruit with a single, smooth stone. The apricot is native to northern China and was known to be a food source as early as 2200 B.C. Apricots are an excellent source of vitamins A and C, potassium, fiber, and iron.

Selection

When choosing apricots, look for those that are well colored, plump, and fairly firm but yield slightly when gently pressed. An apricot that is soft to the touch and juicy is fully ripe and should be eaten right away. If an apricot is hard, it can be placed in a brown paper bag and allowed to ripen at room temperature for a day or two. Refrigerate apricots in the crisper bin of the refrigerator for up to a week. Wash them in cool water just before using.

BANANA

The banana has been around for so long that, according to Hindu legend, it was actually the forbidden fruit of the Garden of Eden. It also is believed that the banana was widely cultivated throughout Asia and Oceania before recorded history and that the Spanish colonists introduced banana shoots to the New World in 1516.

Bananas are reputed to be one of nature's best energy sources and are a rich source of vitamins A, B6, and C as well as fiber. They are ideal fare for postexercise activity because they replace important nutrients, such as potassium, which is often lost during strenuous activity.

Selection

Bananas are picked when they are green and sweeten as they ripen until they get to market. When choosing a banana, look for one that is completely yellow. The riper a banana, or the more yellow its skin, the sweeter it is. Bananas that are yellow but have green tips and green necks or are all yellow with light green necks are ready to eat. Green bananas will ripen at room temperature in two or three days. Alternatively, they can be placed in a brown paper bag to ripen. If an apple is added to the bag, the bananas will ripen even faster. Once ripe, bananas can be stored at room temperature or in the refrigerator for a couple of days.

BLACKBERRY

The blackberry is a small black, blue, or dark-red berry that grows on thorny bushes (brambles). These berries are oblong in shape and grow up to one inch in length. The United States is the world's dominant producer of blackberries. Blackberries are at their peak in flavor and availability from June through September but may still be found in some supermarkets from November into April. They are rich in vitamin C and fiber and a good source of folate.

Selection

When choosing blackberries, look for ones that are plump and solid with full color and a bright, fresh appearance. Place them in a shallow container to prevent the berries on top from crushing those on the bottom and cover the container. They may be stored in the crisper bin of the refrigerator for up to two days. Wash blackberries in cool water just before using.

BLUEBERRY

Native to North America, the blueberry has the distinction of being the second most popular berry in the United States. It has been around for thousands of years but was not cultivated until the turn of the twentieth century. Today, 95% of the world's commercial crop of blueberries is grown in the United States. Blueberries are at their peak in flavor from mid-April to late September. They are available in the southern states first and gradually move north as the season progresses. Blueberries are an excellent source of vitamins A and C as well as fiber.

Selection

When choosing blueberries, look for those that are plump and firm with a dark-blue color and a silvery "bloom" (the powder on blueberries protects them from the sun—it does not rinse off). Avoid any that appear to be dull because this may indicate that the fruit is old. Blueberries should be prepared in the same way as blackberries; however, they can be stored for a longer time in the crisper bin of the refrigerator, from three to five days.

CHERRY

Cherries are small, round, red to black fruit that grow on a tree. There are numerous varieties, but all of them fall into one of three categories: sweet, sour, or a hybrid of the two. Cherries grow in the temperate zones of Europe, Asia, and the Americas. It's believed that they originated in northeastern Asia and later spread throughout the temperate zones in prehistory, carried by birds who ate the cherries and later dropped the stones. Cherries are available from late May through early August. They are a good source of vitamin C and fiber.

Selection

When choosing cherries, look for those that are dark red, plump, and firm, with an attached stem. Store them in the crisper bin of the refrigerator for up to two days and wash them in cool water just before using.

KIWIFRUIT

The kiwifruit (or kiwi) is about the size of a plum and grows on a vine. It has a brown, fuzzy skin and a luscious sweet-and-sour emerald-green pulp that surrounds a cluster of black seeds. Kiwis originated in the 1600s in the Yangtze River valley in China, where it was called "Yangtao." In 1906, Yangtao seeds were sent to New Zealand, where the fruit was renamed "Chinese gooseberry." In 1962, the Chinese gooseberry was shipped to the United States, where it was again renamed the "kiwifruit" in honor of New Zealand's famous national bird. Kiwi is available all year. It's high in vitamin C and fiber and is a good source of vitamin E and potassium.

Selection

When choosing a kiwi, look for one that is light brown, has a sweet aroma, and is firm yet will give slightly when pressed. Kiwi will ripen at room temperature in three to five days. Kiwi also can be placed in a brown paper bag, along with an apple or banana, to speed up the ripening process. When ripe, store kiwi in the crisper bin of the refrigerator for up to three weeks.

LIME

The lime is a small, aromatic fruit with a flavor similar to the lemon except that it's less acidic and more aromatic. It has a smooth, dark-green skin and measures about 1 to 2½ inches in diameter. The lime is native to India and grows in most subtropical regions, such as Mexico and the West Indies. Limes are high in vitamin C and are a good source of fiber.

Selection

To choose a lime with the most juice, look for one that is plump, heavy for its size, firm, and medium to large in size. The skin should be smooth and shiny and deep green in color. Sprinkle limes with a couple of drops of cool water and store them in a resealable plastic bag in the crisper bin of the refrigerator for up to three weeks. Wash them in cool water just before using.

MANGO

Mangoes were cultivated in India and the Malay Archipelago as long as 4,000 years ago. In the 1700s and 1800s, European explorers introduced the fruit to other tropical areas. Mangoes were first raised in the United States sometime in the early 1900s.

The mango resembles a peach in appearance but is more elongated in shape. It has a thin, leathery skin that is waxy and smooth, and its color can be green, red, orange, yellow, or any combination. The skin surrounds a very aromatic and juicy pulp and a hard inner pit. Mangoes are rich in beta-carotene, vitamin C, potassium, and fiber.

Selection

When choosing a mango, look for one that is very fragrant and plump around the stem area and gives slightly when pressed. No matter what the color of the mango, the best-flavored ones will have a yellow tinge when ripe. Mangoes also can be ripened at room temperature. To accelerate the process, place the mango and an apple in a brown paper bag overnight. Once ripened, it can be stored in the crisper bin of the refrigerator for up to five days. Wash in cool water and dry the fruit well just before using.

MELON

Melons, surprisingly, are members of the cucumber family. They grow on vines that can be up to seven feet long. There are two distinct types of melons: muskmelons and watermelons. The muskmelon category includes summer melons (cantaloupe and muskmelon) and winter melons (casaba and honeydew). All melons are high in vitamin C.

Selection

When choosing a melon, look for one that is unblemished, firm, and free of any soft spots. Pick up a few melons and choose the one that is the heaviest for its size. Also, smell the stem end of the melon to see whether it has a fresh, melon aroma. If it has no aroma, the fruit is not ripe. To ripen a melon, place it in a loosely closed brown paper bag. Melons should be washed in cool water and refrigerated until ready to use.

ORANGE

Fresh oranges are widely grown in Florida, California, and Arizona and are available all year long. The two major varieties are the Valencia and the navel. Two other varieties grown in the western states are the Cara Cara and the Moro orange (similar to the blood orange), both of which are available throughout the winter months. Oranges are very high in vitamin C and fiber.

Selection

When selecting an orange, look for one that is firm and heavy for its size. Avoid oranges with a bruised skin, indicating possible fermentation, as well as those with a loose skin, suggesting that they may be dry inside. Although oranges can be stored at room temperature for a few days, their flavor is best when kept refrigerated. Wash oranges in cool water before storing them in the crisper bin of the refrigerator.

PEACH AND NECTARINE

Grown since prehistoric times, peaches were first cultivated in China. They were later introduced into Europe and Persia. It's believed that the Spaniards brought peaches to North, Central, and South America. The Spanish missionaries planted the first peach trees in California.

Numerous varieties of peaches are available, and they are broken down into rough classifications. One type of peach is the "freestone," so named because the pit separates easily from the peach. Another variety is the "clingstone," in which the pit is firmly attached to the fruit. The freestone is the peach most often found in supermarkets because it's easy to eat, while clingstones are frequently canned. Peaches are available almost year-round and are a good source of vitamins A and C as well as fiber.

The nectarine is a smooth-skinned variety of the peach. Nectarines are high in vitamin C and rich in vitamin A and fiber.

Selection

When choosing nectarines, look for those with bright-red markings over a yellow skin. Avoid any with wrinkled skin or those that are soft and bruised. The nectarine should yield gently to the touch and have a sweet aroma. To ripen nectarines, place them in a brown paper bag and keep at room temperature. Once ripe, store them in a single layer in the crisper bin for up to one week. Wash nectarines in cool water just before using.

When picking peaches, look for ones that are relatively firm with a fuzzy, creamy yellow skin and a sweet aroma. The pink blush on the peach indicates its variety, not its ripeness. Avoid peaches with a wrinkled skin or those that are soft or blemished. The peach should yield gently when touched. To ripen peaches, keep them at room temperature and out of direct sun until they yield slightly to the touch. Once ripe, store them in a single layer in the crisper bin of the refrigerator for up to five days. Wash peaches in cool water just before using.

PEAR

Pear is the name of a tree of the rose family and its fruit. It's believed that pears were eaten by Stone Age people; however, the pears we are accustomed to eating were first cultivated in southeastern Europe and western Asia around 2000 B.C. Pear trees were introduced to the Americas when European settlers arrived in the 1700s. Pears are a source of vitamin C, fiber, and potassium.

Selection

Pears are a unique fruit because they ripen best off the tree. This explains why they are often so hard when purchased at the supermarket. Many pears have stickers that tell you the stage of ripeness, such as "ready to eat" or "let me ripen for two days." When choosing pears, look for ones that are firm and unblemished with a fresh pear aroma. To ripen pears, place them in a brown paper bag at room temperature for a few days. When they yield to gentle thumb pressure, pears are ready to eat. Once ripe, wash pears in cool water and store them in the crisper bin of the refrigerator for two to five days.

PINEAPPLE

The pineapple is a tropical fruit that is native to Central and South America. In 1493, Christopher Columbus discovered pineapples growing on the island of Guadeloupe and brought them back to Spain. By the 1700s, pineapples were being grown in greenhouses throughout Europe. They are an excellent source of vitamin C.

Selection

When choosing a pineapple, look for one that has a fresh pineapple aroma and a crown with crisp, fresh-looking green leaves and a brightly colored shell. It also should be heavy and symmetrical in size. Avoid any pineapples that have soft spots or are discolored. To store a pineapple, cut the fruit from the shell and refrigerate it in an airtight container for up to one week.

PLUM

Wild plums have been around for so long that they were gathered by our prehistoric ancestors. Later, it's believed that cultivated plum plants were introduced in ancient Rome from Damascus. Today, 200 to 300 varieties of plums are grown in the United States. They come in a wide variety of colors, ranging from purple and red to yellow, green, and blue. The Damson, which is small and oval and has a tart flavor, is the family to which several varieties of common garden plums belong. Plums are rich in vitamin C.

Selection

Choose a plum that has good color; is heavy for its size; and has a sweet, familiar plum fragrance. The fruit should yield slightly to pressure, especially close to the stem end. Avoid any plums that are too soft, have a shriveled skin, exhibit brown spots, or show any sign of leakage. If the plum is hard, it will ripen in a brown paper bag at room temperature after a few days. Wash plums well in cool water and store them in a single layer in the crisper bin of the refrigerator for up to five days.

RASPBERRY

It's believed that red raspberries spread all over Europe and Asia in prehistoric times. Because they were so delicious growing wild, it was not until the 1600s that raspberries were cultivated in Europe. Those that are cultivated in North America originated from two groups: the red raspberry, native to Europe, and the wild red variety, native to North America. Raspberries are an excellent source of vitamin C, fiber, and folate.

Selection

When choosing raspberries, it's always best to buy them when they are in season, usually starting in late June and lasting four to six weeks. If you're fortunate enough to have a local berry farm, take advantage of it by visiting at the beginning of the season to get the best pick. Select berries that are large and plump, bright, shiny, uniform in color, and free of mold. Avoid any that are mushy. Before refrigerating raspberries, carefully go through the batch and discard any that show signs of spoilage. Place the raspberries in a shallow container to prevent the berries on top from crushing those on the bottom and cover the container. They may be stored in the crisper bin of the refrigerator for up to two days. Wash raspberries in a gentle stream of cool water just before you're ready to use them.

STRAWBERRY

Strawberries date as far back as 2,200 years ago. They are known to have grown wild in Italy in the third century, and by 1588 they were discovered in Virginia by the first European settlers. Local Indians cultivated the strawberry as early as the mid-1600s, and by the middle of the nineteenth century, this fruit was widely grown in many parts of North America.

The strawberry grows in groups of three on the stem of a plant that is very low to the ground. As the fruit ripens, it changes from greenish white in color to a lush flame red. The strawberry does not have a skin but is actually covered by hundreds of tiny seeds. Strawberries are a rich source of vitamin C and fiber.

Selection

The best time to buy strawberries is in June and July, when they are at their peak of juicy freshness. As with raspberries, if you're lucky enough to live near a strawberry farm, a "pick your own" day trip is a wonderful family outing as well as an excellent way to get the very best of the crop. Look for plump, firm, and deep-colored fruit with a bright-green cap and a sweet strawberry aroma. Strawberries can be stored in a single layer in the crisper bin of the refrigerator for up to two days. Wash them with their caps in a gentle stream of cool water just before you're ready to use them.

FREEZING FRUIT

To make a smoothie with the optimal consistency, it's important that the fresh fruit you use has been frozen for 30 minutes or more. Using frozen fruit also helps maintain your smoothie at an ideal icy-cold temperature. Another reason you may want to freeze fruit is simply to store it for later use. This is especially useful when you know that certain seasonal fruits will no longer be available after a certain date. By purchasing an ample quantity to freeze, you can be certain of having a supply on hand when you need it to prepare one of your favorite smoothies. Also, there may be times when already ripened fruit isn't needed immediately, so freezing prevents overripening and allows it to be utilized at a later time.

Whether you're freezing for immediate use or for storage, the basic preparation is identical.

- When ready to freeze cherries and apricots (which should be cut in half and their stones removed) or berries, place them in a colander and rinse with a gentle stream of cool water. Pat them dry with a paper towel.

- To freeze a plum, peach, nectarine (remove its stone), or pear (remove its stem and seeds), cut them into small pieces.

- For a banana or kiwifruit, remove its skin and either slice it or freeze it whole and then slice it later before use.

- Before freezing oranges and limes, remove the peel and pith, break each into segments, and remove any seeds.

- To prepare apples, mangoes, and melons for freezing, remove their peels and seeds or pits before cubing.

- When ready to freeze a pineapple, remove its top, the outer layering, and the core, then cut into cubes.

Place prepared fruit on a baking sheet lined with parchment or waxed paper and freeze it for 30 minutes or longer, after which time it will be ready to add to the other smoothie ingredients. If frozen fruit is to be used at a later date, transfer the frozen pieces to an airtight plastic bag large enough to hold them in a single layer. Label and mark the date on the bag and freeze for up to two weeks. Most fruit can be kept in the freezer this long without a loss of flavor.

Getting Started– Making a Summer Smoothie

Equipment and Techniques

Aside from the fabulous taste, another unique attraction of smoothies is that they're unbelievably quick and easy to prepare. With many of us feeling overbooked with life's daily responsibilities, the last thing we want to do is to spend a lot of time in the kitchen. Enter the classic smoothie. With very little effort, you can enjoy a satisfying and richly flavored drink within minutes. With such an unbeatable combination of good taste and ease of preparation, it's no wonder smoothies have quickly become one of the ultimate culinary rages of our era.

All that's needed to accomplish this miracle of flavors is a modest number of essential tools to equip your smoothie station: a sharp knife for prepping fruit, a rubber spatula to remove every last drop from the blender, airtight freezer bags for storing freshly cut fruit in the freezer, and, of course, the invaluable blender. There are, in addition, a few optional items of equipment. As you glance through the garnish recipes found in this cookbook, you'll note that some of them suggest using a silicone mat, which is a reusable laminated food-grade silicone sheet that prevents food from sticking during the baking process. This is a very useful item but not an absolute necessity. Finally, although a food processor can be used to make a smoothie, most smoothie mavens would agree that a blender definitely is the preferred appliance. While a food processor can be used to puree fruit and ice, it often leaves small chunks of ice. On the other hand, a blender breaks up the ice and fruit into tiny particles and is better able to process liquids and solids into a fine, smooth, and well-aerated puree.

EQUIPMENT

A blender is the most important piece of kitchen equipment you'll need to make a proper smoothie. The invention of this indispensable appliance is credited to Stephen J. Poplawski, who, in 1922, first conceived of placing a spinning blade at the bottom of a glass container. By 1935, Fred Waring and Frederick Osius made significant improvements on the original design and began marketing the "Waring blender." The rest is history.

A blender basically consists of a tall and narrow stainless-steel, plastic, or glass food container fitted with metal blades at the bottom. These blades usually have four cutting edges placed on two or four planes, allowing the ingredients in the container to hit multiple cutting surfaces. An upward motion is caused by the rapidly spinning blades, creating a vortex in the container that allows for the incorporation of more air in the final product, giving it a smoother consistency.

When selecting a blender, you should assess certain basic qualities, including its durability, ease of operation and cleaning, capacity, and noise production. With such a wide variety of blenders from which to choose, I hope the following information will help you narrow your choice.

- Blender containers typically come in two sizes: 32 ounces and 40 ounces. If you'll routinely be preparing smoothies for more than two people, choose the larger one.

- Blender motors come in different sizes. Those with 290-watt motors are adequate for most blending jobs but are not optimal for smoothies. Others with 330- to 400-watt motors are considered to be of professional caliber and are excellent for crushing ice, a feature that is very important for creating the best smoothies.

- Blenders can be found with a variety of blade speed options, ranging from two (high and low) to multiple (between 5 and 14) speeds. Variable-speed models provide more options, such as the ability to liquefy and whip.

- The blender should have a removable bottom for ease of cleaning.

- Container lids should have a secondary lid that can be easily removed. This allows for the addition of ingredients while the blender is turned on.

- Avoid plastic container jars because they become scratched over time and do not wash well in the dishwasher.

Recently, a new blender that was specifically designed to make smoothies has become available. This whirring wizard, called the Smoothie Elite (by Back to Basics), has several features, including a custom stir stick to break up the air pockets, an ice-crunching blade that ensures consistent smoothie texture, and a convenient spigot at the bottom of the container that serves up the finished product.

Although a blender is the ideal appliance for making smoothies, you may prefer a food processor because of its overall versatility or, more important, because it's an appliance that you already own. The *New York Times* described the food processor as the "twentieth-century French revolution." This unique appliance can mince, chop, grate, shred, slice, knead, blend, puree, liquefy, and crush ice.

The food processor has a base directly under the work bowl that houses the motor. A metal shaft extending from the base through the center of the work bowl connects the blade or disc to the motor. A cover that fits over the work bowl has a feed tube. When the bowl is locked into place and the motor is switched on, the

shaft turns and propels the blades or discs. Un-
like the blender container, the food processor
bowl is wide and low, causing food to be sent
sideways rather than upward by the spinning
blade. This motion results in food striking the
sides of the container, with less incorporation of
air than in the upward motion produced by a
blender.

Similar to the blender, the food processor
has some basic features you should assess when
attempting to select the one that will best fit
your cooking needs.

- Food processors come in a wide range of
  sizes. The 2- or 3-cup miniprocessor is practi-
  cal for chopping, especially small quantities of
  food. Those with 7-, 9-, and 11-cup capacities
  are each equally suitable for making smoothies
  as well as other food preparations, while 14-
  and 20-cup units are ideal for professional
  cooking needs.

- Although a few food processors have four
  speeds, most have two (high and low) in addition to a pulsing action.

- Some food processors come with both large
  and small feed tubes. The larger tube is convenient when large-size ingredients are to be
  added while the machine is running.

Once you've decided on the features you would
like in a blender (or food processor), I highly rec-
ommend that you visit several appliance or department stores and personally view the various
models available. The salesclerk should be able to
provide you with information to further help you

in making the best decision. Another resource for gleaning valuable information is the Internet. Many of the companies that manufacture these appliances have sites that are quite informative, and some also provide a phone number so that you can personally speak to a representative. Finally, *Consumer Reports* and similar publications provide comparison quality ratings for a variety of blenders and food processors.

HELPFUL TECHNIQUES

Now that the blender has taken its rightful place—center stage on your countertop—it's time to rev it up and make a smoothie. Equipping your kitchen with the necessary tools to make smoothies was relatively easy, and you'll be pleased to learn that mastering the techniques required to prepare them is just as simple. In fact, preparing a smoothie is probably one of the most uncomplicated tasks you'll ever have to perform in your kitchen. Simply place all the appropriate smoothie ingredients in a blender, and you'll end up with a perfectly acceptable final product. However, for those who want to create the ultimate smoothie, there are a few helpful techniques that will help you reach that lofty goal.

- To ensure having the most delicious fruit, buy it when it's in season and at its peak flavor.

- Before freezing fruit, wash and dry it first, then follow the preparation instructions given in chapter 2.

- When ready to freeze the fruit, set it in a shallow pan lined with a piece of parchment (or waxed) paper to prevent it from sticking to the surface. Place the fruit in the freezer for at least 30 minutes or until partially frozen. Using frozen fruit ensures that the smoothie will have a thick consistency and also be icy cold.

- Store-bought individually frozen fruit can be substituted for fresh frozen fruit, but it should be used within six months of the purchase date. Avoid using frozen fruit that is packaged in sweetened syrup.

- To be certain that you have a supply of your favorite seasonal fruits, stock up before they are no longer available for purchase. Although fruits have the most flavor when kept frozen for only one to two weeks, they can be kept in the freezer for a slightly longer amount of time.

- If you're using ice in a smoothie, the individual pieces should be slightly smaller than the cut-up fruit to prevent any chunks of ice remaining once the smoothie is blended. If you don't own a high-speed blender, you can make your own crushed ice simply by placing ice cubes in a resealable bag and crushing them with a mallet or rolling pin. An easier alternative to cutting the ice is to buy a bag of ice chips or crushed ice to keep in your freezer.

- Fill mini ice-cube trays with orange, lemon, lime, pineapple, or apple juice to create frozen juice cubes. Commercial juice works fine, but if the opportunity presents itself, use freshly squeezed varieties instead. These cubes make a flavorful alternative to plain ice cubes because they infuse additional rich fruity flavor to smoothies.

- When adding ingredients to a blender, always add the chilled liquid first, then the frozen fruit, and the ice or frozen yogurt last. Start the blender on low speed to crush the ice and fruit and blend the mixture. Gradually increase the speed until the mixture is smooth. It may be necessary to turn the blender off periodically and stir the mixture with a spoon, working from the bottom up.

- If the smoothie is too thin, add more fruit or ice. Conversely, if the smoothie is too thick, add more liquid.

CHAPTER 4

Simple Pleasures

All-Time Summer Favorites

Smoothies are undoubtedly one of the most popular and refreshing taste treats to have emerged in recent years. The ones described in this chapter, made with a simple combination of fresh fruits and juices, are a healthy, lowfat, and delicious alternative to more fat- and calorie-laden blended drinks, such as malts, milk shakes, and blizzards. What's even more exciting about these sensational fruity concoctions is that the combination of ingredients you choose to create them is limited only by your imagination.

As you browse through this chapter, you'll be impressed with the great variety of fruit-and-juice combinations that are possible and with the delightful result that each recipe provides. Be ready to be impressed when you try *Give Peach a*

Chance, a refreshing smoothie made with peaches, banana, and orange juice. If tropical flavors suit you more, you'll be thrilled with the summer taste of *Stand by Your Mango,* a delicious blend of mango, apricot, banana, and honey.

I hope that as you prepare smoothies from the recipes provided in this chapter, you'll feel encouraged to experiment with some of your own favorite fruit combinations. Once you have "tasted" success, nothing will stand in the way of creating your own signature smoothie.

Berry the Hatchet

This unadorned blueberry and mango smoothie, with its blatant blue color, is definitely a class act. Serve it at teatime with a basket of mini blueberry muffins.

1 SERVING

⅔ cup orange juice

1 tablespoon honey

1 cup diced mango

½ cup blackberries

½ cup diced banana

Place the orange juice, honey, mango, blackberries, and banana in a blender and mix on low speed until the mixture is blended. Continue mixing, gradually increasing the speed, until the mixture is smooth. Pour the smoothie into a glass and garnish with Blackberries on a Skewer (see page 194), if desired.

Calories	352.50	Protein	3.35 g
Calories from fat	12.75	Total fat	1.42 g
Carbohydrates	89.46 g	Fiber	8.96 g
Calcium	63.50 g	Iron	1.28 mg
Potassium	1037.20 mg	Beta-carotene	3983.16 mcg
Magnesium	69.61 mg	Vitamin C	150.42 mg

Blue Mango Group

If you're an angry convert from fat- and calorie-rich drinks like milk shakes, let bygones be bygones and just enjoy this refreshing, healthful mix of blueberry, mango, and banana.

1 SERVING

⅔ cup pineapple juice

1 ½ tablespoons honey

1 cup blueberries

½ cup diced mango

½ cup diced banana

Place the pineapple juice, honey, blueberries, mango, and banana in a blender and mix on low speed until the mixture is blended. Continue mixing, gradually increasing the speed, until the mixture is smooth. Pour the smoothie into a glass and garnish with a Pineapple Bow (see page 206), if desired.

Calories	387.11	Protein	2.26 g
Calories from fat	10.20	Total fat	1.13 g
Carbohydrates	98.27 g	Fiber	7.26 g
Calcium	23.36 g	Iron	0.72 mg
Potassium	777.94 mg	Beta-carotene	2110.55 mcg
Magnesium	37.06 mg	Vitamin C	88.69 mg

Bye-Bye Blackberry

It's true! After one stimulating glassful of this re-freshing blackberry, apricot, and banana smoothie, you can pack up all your cares and woes.

1 SERVING

⅔ cup orange juice

1½ tablespoons honey

1 cup blackberries

½ cup diced apricot

½ cup diced banana

Place the orange juice, honey, blackberries, apricot, and banana in a blender and mix on low speed until the mixture is blended. Continue mixing, gradually increasing the speed, until the mixture is smooth. Pour the smoothie into a glass and garnish with a sprig of fresh mint (see page 205), if desired.

Calories	354.50	Protein	4.22 g
Calories from fat	14.17	Total fat	1.57 g
Carbohydrates	88.50 g	Fiber	11.81 g
Calcium	82.22 g	Iron	1.96 mg
Potassium	1170.63 mg	Beta-carotene	1451.15 mcg
Magnesium	75.97 mg	Vitamin C	128.14 mg

California Whirls

You may have several smoothie favorites, but once you sample this fruit-filled delight, you may find yourself wishing they could all be California Whirls. Fill a thermos with this refreshing elixir before you head for the waves.

1 SERVING

½ cup apricot nectar

1 tablespoon honey

½ cup diced strawberries

½ cup diced pineapple

½ cup diced banana

Place the apricot nectar, honey, strawberries, pineapple, and banana in a blender and mix on low speed until the mixture is blended. Continue mixing, gradually increasing the speed, until the mixture is smooth. Pour the smoothie into a glass and garnish with a Pineapple Chip (see page 207), if desired.

Calories	264.47	Protein	2.07 g
Calories from fat	9.79	Total fat	1.09 g
Carbohydrates	68.03 g	Fiber	5.27 g
Calcium	30.62 g	Iron	1.37 mg
Potassium	664.82 mg	Beta-carotene	1045.06 mcg
Magnesium	46.90 mg	Vitamin C	62.71 mg

Chill Out

According to the Oxford Dictionary of Slang, *to chill out means "to become less tense or to relax." According to* Summer Smoothies, *it means "to enjoy a delicious cold combination of bananas, strawberries, and honey with orange and pineapple juice."*

1 SERVING

¾ cup pineapple juice

1 tablespoon honey

1 cup diced banana

½ cup diced strawberries

½ cup frozen mini orange-juice cubes

Place the pineapple juice, honey, banana, strawberries, and orange-juice cubes in a blender and mix on low speed until the mixture is blended. Continue mixing, gradually increasing the speed, until the mixture is smooth. Pour the smoothie into a glass and garnish with a Pineapple Spear (see page 209), if desired.

Calories	378.51	Protein	2.94 g
Calories from fat	11.24	Total fat	1.25 g
Carbohydrates	93.33 g	Fiber	5.64 g
Calcium	34.55 g	Iron	1.09 mg
Potassium	1211.68 mg	Beta-carotene	200.19 mcg
Magnesium	65.16 mg	Vitamin C	163.85 mg

Daytona Peach

It will be a race to the finish in your house to see who gets to taste this prize-winning combination of peaches, strawberries, and blackberries first. Serve along with your own checkered flag made with a bowlful of black and white jellybeans.

1 SERVING

⅔ cup peach nectar

1 ½ tablespoons honey

1 cup diced peach

½ cup diced strawberries

½ cup blackberries

Place the peach nectar, honey, peach, strawberries, and blackberries in a blender and mix on low speed until the mixture is blended. Continue mixing, gradually increasing the speed, until the mixture is smooth. Pour the smoothie into a glass and garnish the rim with a Strawberry Fan (see page 215), if desired.

Calories	321.69	Protein	2.76 g
Calories from fat	6.97	Total fat	0.77 g
Carbohydrates	83.18 g	Fiber	10.18 g
Calcium	53.37 g	Iron	1.36 mg
Potassium	696.73 mg	Beta-carotene	708.86 mcg
Magnesium	41.88 mg	Vitamin C	82.36 mg

Equal Opportunity Blender

Anyone who loves smoothies will have interest in this fruit-filled creation. You can bank on it.

1 SERVING

½ cup pineapple juice

1 tablespoon honey

½ cup diced cherries

½ cup diced banana

½ cup raspberries

½ cup frozen mini orange-juice cubes

Place the pineapple juice, honey, cherries, banana, raspberries, and orange-juice cubes in a blender and mix on low speed until the mixture is blended. Continue mixing, gradually increasing the speed, until the mixture is smooth. Pour the smoothie into a glass and garnish with a Pineapple Wedge (see page 209), if desired.

Calories	336.55	Protein	3.13 g
Calories from fat	14.78	Total fat	1.64 g
Carbohydrates	82.04 g	Fiber	7.94 g
Calcium	43.82 g	Iron	1.20 mg
Potassium	966.90 mg	Beta-carotene	236.64 mcg
Magnesium	54.86 mg	Vitamin C	119.38 mg

Fla-mango

No castanets are needed to create this seductively delicious mango and apricot smoothie. Just stomp your heels, flick on the blender, and listen to the olé's! It's the perfect accompaniment to your next tapas party.

1 SERVING

⅔ cup orange juice

1 ½ tablespoons honey

1 cup diced mango

½ cup diced apricots

Place the orange juice, honey, mango, and apricots in a blender and mix on low speed until the mixture is blended. Continue mixing, gradually increasing the speed, until the mixture is smooth. Pour the smoothie into a glass and garnish the rim with a Lime Wheel (see page 202), if desired.

Calories	317.87	Protein	3.25 g
Calories from fat	9.88	Total fat	1.10 g
Carbohydrates	80.61 g	Fiber	5.34 g
Calcium	48.14 g	Iron	1.12 mg
Potassium	848.79 mg	Beta-carotene	5197.13 mcg
Magnesium	40.27 mg	Vitamin C	136.78 mg

Fruit for Thought

Scratch your chin, give your blender a spin, and then contemplate how wonderful life is while enjoying this heavenly combination of fruits and fruit juices.

1 SERVING

½ cup pineapple juice

1 tablespoon honey

½ cup diced cantaloupe

½ cup diced peach

½ cup diced banana

½ cup frozen mini orange-juice cubes

Place the pineapple juice, honey, cantaloupe, peach, banana, and orange-juice cubes in a blender and mix on low speed until the mixture is blended. Continue mixing, gradually increasing the speed, until the mixture is smooth. Pour the smoothie into a glass and garnish with a Pineapple Bow (see page 206), if desired.

Calories	318.76	Protein	3.00 g
Calories from fat	8.18	Total fat	0.91 g
Carbohydrates	79.05 g	Fiber	4.43 g
Calcium	32.46 g	Iron	0.83 mg
Potassium	1125.67 mg	Beta-carotene	1890.47 mcg
Magnesium	50.56 mg	Vitamin C	138.30 mg

Give Peach a Chance

Are apples your favorite fruit? Are you more of a grapefruit person? In either case, you may want to reconsider. With this classic smoothie recipe, all I'm saying is, give peach a chance.

1 SERVING

½ cup orange juice

½ tablespoon honey

1 cup diced peach

½ cup diced banana

Place the orange juice, honey, peach, and banana in a blender and mix on low speed until the mixture is blended. Continue mixing, gradually increasing the speed, until the mixture is smooth. Pour the smoothie into a glass and garnish with a Fruit Skewer (see page 200), if desired.

Calories	230.10	Protein	2.86 g
Calories from fat	6.85	Total fat	0.76 g
Carbohydrates	58.07 g	Fiber	5.47 g
Calcium	27.28 g	Iron	0.71 mg
Potassium	885.41 mg	Beta-carotene	533.82 mcg
Magnesium	47.50 mg	Vitamin C	80.10 mg

Lime All Shook Up

Once your blender is swiveling faster than the King, you'll fall in love with this tart little smoothie. Sample this light and refreshing concoction after a brisk workout.

1 SERVING

⅔ cup apricot nectar

1½ tablespoons honey

1 cup diced banana

½ cup diced apricots

½ cup frozen mini lime-juice cubes

Place the apricot nectar, honey, banana, apricots, and lime-juice cubes in a blender and mix on low speed until the mixture is blended. Continue mixing, gradually increasing the speed, until the mixture is smooth. Pour the smoothie into a glass and garnish the rim with a Lime Wheel (see page 202), if desired.

Calories	401.13	Protein	3.96 g
Calories from fat	11.84	Total fat	1.32 g
Carbohydrates	105.67 g	Fiber	7.14 g
Calcium	45.24 g	Iron	1.72 mg
Potassium	1179.56 mg	Beta-carotene	2680.20 mcg
Magnesium	66.48 mg	Vitamin C	59.10 mg

Little Surfer Whirl

Make this delicious fruit-filled smoothie for some friends, and you're certain to be catchin' a rave.

1 SERVING

⅔ cup peach nectar

1 ½ tablespoons honey

½ cup diced cantaloupe

½ cup blueberries

½ cup raspberries

Place the peach nectar, honey, cantaloupe, blueberries, and raspberries in a blender and mix on low speed until the mixture is blended. Continue mixing, gradually increasing the speed, until the mixture is smooth. Pour the smoothie into a glass and garnish with Berries on a Skewer (see page 194), if desired.

Calories	284.99	Protein	2.29 g
Calories from fat	7.84	Total fat	0.87 g
Carbohydrates	73.34 g	Fiber	7.84 g
Calcium	36.89 g	Iron	1.09 mg
Potassium	488.13 mg	Beta-carotene	1812.65 mcg
Magnesium	30.77 mg	Vitamin C	67.52 mg

Macho, Macho Mango

You can enjoy this delicious combination of mango, banana, and strawberries in the country, the city, or the "village," "people." Better yet, invite your tennis partners over to cool down with a glass-ful of this fruit-filled delight.

1 SERVING

⅔ cup pineapple juice

1 tablespoon honey

1 cup diced mango

½ cup diced banana

½ cup diced strawberries

Place the pineapple juice, honey, mango, banana, and strawberries in a blender and mix on low speed until the mixture is blended. Continue mixing, gradually increasing the speed, until the mixture is smooth. Pour the smoothie into a glass and garnish with a Pineapple Spear (see page 209), if desired.

Calories	352.23	Protein	2.18 g
Calories from fat	10.01	Total fat	1.11 g
Carbohydrates	88.91 g	Fiber	6.72 g
Calcium	33.89 g	Iron	0.85 mg
Potassium	909.86 mg	Beta-carotene	3962.55 mcg
Magnesium	45.32 mg	Vitamin C	139.70 mg

Mango Overboard

S.O.S. (Special Occasion Smoothie). There'll be no mutiny over this mango, raspberry, and banana flavored bounty. For an afternoon break, serve alongside a plate of sugar cookies.

1 SERVING

⅔ cup orange juice

1 tablespoon honey

1 cup diced mango

½ cup diced banana

½ cup raspberries

Place the orange juice, honey, mango, banana, and raspberries in a blender and mix on low speed until the mixture is blended. Continue mixing, gradually increasing the speed, until the mixture is smooth. Pour the smoothie into a glass and garnish with Berries on a Skewer (see page 94), if desired.

Calories	345.19	Protein	3.39 g
Calories from fat	13.27	Total fat	1.47 g
Carbohydrates	87.39 g	Fiber	9.33 g
Calcium	53.99 g	Iron	1.22 mg
Potassium	989.56 mg	Beta-carotene	3972.59 mcg
Magnesium	66.28 mg	Vitamin C	150.68 mg

Melon-choly Baby

One taste of this richly flavored cantaloupe, raspberry, and banana treat is more than enough to chase the blues away. So invite some friends over for a casual gathering and serve this refreshing smoothie. They'll all be happy you did.

1 SERVING

⅔ cup orange juice

1½ tablespoons honey

1 cup diced cantaloupe

½ cup raspberries

½ cup diced banana

Place the orange juice, honey, cantaloupe, raspberries, and banana in a blender and mix on low speed until the mixture is blended. Continue mixing, gradually increasing the speed, until the mixture is smooth. Pour the smoothie into a glass and garnish with a Crisp Banana Wafer (see page 198), if desired.

Calories	326.15	Protein	3.99 g
Calories from fat	13.29	Total fat	1.48 g
Carbohydrates	81.45 g	Fiber	7.66 g
Calcium	55.72 g	Iron	1.38 mg
Potassium	1232.07 mg	Beta-carotene	3193.49 mcg
Magnesium	69.24 mg	Vitamin C	172.55 mg

One in a Melon

What are the chances that you won't enjoy this pleasingly sweet combination of cantaloupe, orange, and apple flavors? The name says it all.

1 SERVING

½ cup apple juice

1 tablespoon honey

½ teaspoon vanilla extract

1 cup diced cantaloupe

½ cup frozen mini orange-juice cubes

Place the apple juice, honey, vanilla, cantaloupe, and orange-juice cubes in a blender and mix on low speed until the mixture is blended. Continue mixing, gradually increasing the speed, until the mixture is smooth. Pour the smoothie into a glass and garnish with an Apple Chip (see page 192), if desired.

Calories	240.73	Protein	2.42 g
Calories from fat	7.50	Total fat	0.83 g
Carbohydrates	58.49 g	Fiber	1.69 g
Calcium	41.43 g	Iron	1.13 mg
Potassium	904.18 mg	Beta-carotene	3118.63 mcg
Magnesium	35.64 mg	Vitamin C	130.74 mg

Or-anged Marriage

This blissful union of fruits and juices will make a much more appealing start to your breakfast than a ho-hum glass of orange juice.

1 SERVING

⅓ cup apple juice

1 tablespoon honey

½ cup diced banana

¾ cup frozen mini orange-juice cubes

Place the apple juice, honey, banana, and orange-juice cubes in a blender and mix on low speed until the mixture is blended. Continue mixing, gradually increasing the speed, until the mixture is smooth. Pour the smoothie into a glass and garnish the rim with an Orange Wheel (see page 202), if desired.

Calories	255.96	Protein	2.19 g
Calories from fat	7.41	Total fat	0.82 g
Carbohydrates	64.03 g	Fiber	2.30 g
Calcium	32.02 g	Iron	1.00 mg
Potassium	778.39 mg	Beta-carotene	105.53 mcg
Magnesium	45.11 mg	Vitamin C	100.67 mg

Orange-utan

Start the morning with a glassful of this tangy orange and mango smoothie, and you'll be swinging the rest of the day.

1 SERVING

⅔ cup orange juice

1½ tablespoons honey

1 cup diced orange

½ cup diced mango

Place the orange juice, honey, orange, and mango in a blender and mix on low speed until the mixture is blended. Continue mixing, gradually increasing the speed, until the mixture is smooth. Pour the smoothie into a glass and garnish with a Fruit Skewer (see page 200), if desired.

Calories	300.54	Protein	3.37 g
Calories from fat	6.32	Total fat	0.70 g
Carbohydrates	76.60 g	Fiber	5.84 g
Calcium	94.34 g	Iron	0.77 mg
Potassium	769.59 mg	Beta-carotene	2042.33 mcg
Magnesium	42.75 mg	Vitamin C	200.22 mg

Out of Apricot

I'm not "lion" when I predict that this apricot, peach, and banana smoothie will be the "mane" attraction of your lunch or snack. You'll be wild about it.

1 SERVING

²⁄₃ cup apricot nectar

1 ½ tablespoons honey

1 ¼ cups diced apricots

½ cup diced peach

½ cup diced banana

½ cup frozen mini orange-juice cubes

Place the apricot nectar, honey, apricots, peach, banana, and orange-juice cubes in a blender and mix on low speed until the mixture is blended. Continue mixing, gradually increasing the speed, until the mixture is smooth. Pour the smoothie into a glass and garnish with a sprig of fresh mint (see page 205), if desired.

Calories	450.67	Protein	5.84 g
Calories from fat	14.76	Total fat	1.64 g
Carbohydrates	113.11 g	Fiber	9.77 g
Calcium	64.89 g	Iron	2.46 mg
Potassium	1530.24 mg	Beta-carotene	4836.20 mcg
Magnesium	66.84 mg	Vitamin C	96.22 mg

Pango Pango Mango

This Polynesian refresher is so pleasingly sweet that your family is certain to ask for Samoa. Serve with fingers of thinly sliced banana bread.

1 SERVING

⅔ cup pineapple juice

1 tablespoon honey

1 cup diced mango

½ cup diced pineapple

½ cup diced kiwi

Place the pineapple juice, honey, mango, pineapple, and kiwi in a blender and mix on low speed until the mixture is blended. Continue mixing, gradually increasing the speed, until the mixture is smooth. Pour the smoothie into a glass and garnish with a Pineapple Spear (see page 209), if desired.

Calories	350.29	Protein	2.08 g
Calories from fat	10.51	Total fat	1.17 g
Carbohydrates	88.28 g	Fiber	6.95 g
Calcium	46.21 g	Iron	0.95 mg
Potassium	856.48 mg	Beta-carotene	4017.75 mcg
Magnesium	52.67 mg	Vitamin C	184.48 mg

Peached Blond

One sip of this delicious peach, pineapple, and banana smoothie, and your family and friends will be asking, "Does she or doesn't she intend to make another batch of this summer ambrosia?"

1 SERVING

⅔ cup pineapple juice

1½ tablespoons honey

1 cup diced peach

½ cup diced pineapple

½ cup diced banana

Place the pineapple juice, honey, peach, pineapple, and banana in a blender and mix on low speed until the mixture is blended. Continue mixing, gradually increasing the speed, until the mixture is smooth. Pour the smoothie into a glass and garnish with a Pineapple Chip (see page 207), if desired.

Calories	363.36	Protein	2.36 g
Calories from fat	7.62	Total fat	0.85 g
Carbohydrates	92.23 g	Fiber	6.19 g
Calcium	20.33 g	Iron	0.84 mg
Potassium	942.67 mg	Beta-carotene	558.76 mcg
Magnesium	45.14 mg	Vitamin C	70.14 mg

Pineapple Dipporatus

This smoothie is dedicated to my son, David, who is the only one who knows what a dipporatus is. Even if you never find out what it means, you'll be delighted with this rich and creamy pineapple, mango, and peach smoothie.

1 SERVING

⅔ cup peach nectar

1 tablespoon honey

1 cup diced pineapple

½ cup diced mango

½ cup diced peach

Place the peach nectar, honey, pineapple, mango, and peach in a blender and mix on low speed until the mixture is blended. Continue mixing, gradually increasing the speed, until the mixture is smooth. Pour the smoothie into a glass and garnish with a Pineapple Bow (see page 206), if desired.

Calories	320.18	Protein	2.13 g
Calories from fat	8.99	Total fat	1.00 g
Carbohydrates	83.23 g	Fiber	6.08 g
Calcium	32.92 g	Iron	1.18 mg
Potassium	548.72 mg	Beta-carotene	2378.69 mcg
Magnesium	42.14 mg	Vitamin C	61.24 mg

Pineapple Pixel

Invite friends over to watch home videos and indulge in this rich and creamy pineapple smoothie. It does not need to be programmed for color, but its overall image can be enhanced with a simple sprig of mint.

1 SERVING

⅔ cup orange juice

1 tablespoon honey

1 cup diced pineapple

½ cup diced banana

Place the orange juice, honey, pineapple, and banana in a blender and mix on low speed until the mixture is blended. Continue mixing, gradually increasing the speed, until the mixture is smooth. Pour the smoothie into a glass and garnish with a sprig of fresh mint (see page 205), if desired.

Calories	283.76	Protein	2.60 g
Calories from fat	12.21	Total fat	1.36 g
Carbohydrates	71.43 g	Fiber	4.03 g
Calcium	34.81 g	Iron	1.23 mg
Potassium	813.83 mg	Beta-carotene	115.64 mcg
Magnesium	62.06 mg	Vitamin C	113.47 mg

Pineapplesmoothie .com

Looking for a break from surfing the Web? Try a glass of this flavorful pineapple smoothie and then read the following message on the toolbar across the top of your screen: "This smoothie is destined to become a <u>Favorite</u> way to <u>Refresh</u> yourself at <u>Home</u>."

1 SERVING

⅔ cup pineapple juice

1 tablespoon honey

1 cup diced pineapple

½ cup diced cantaloupe

½ cup blueberries

Place the pineapple juice, honey, pineapple, cantaloupe, and blueberries in a blender and mix on low speed until the mixture is blended. Continue mixing, gradually increasing the speed, until the mixture is smooth. Pour the smoothie into a glass and garnish with Berries on a Skewer (see page 194), if desired.

Calories	295.63	Protein	1.86 g
Calories from fat	10.49	Total fat	1.17 g
Carbohydrates	73.60 g	Fiber	4.50 g
Calcium	25.27 g	Iron	0.95 mg
Potassium	704.56 mg	Beta-carotene	1659.64 mcg
Magnesium	34.56 mg	Vitamin C	107.16 mg

Plum and Plummer

To avoid an overly crunchy smoothie, be certain to remove the pits from the plums before placing them in the blender. (Duh!) Serve this fruity blend for breakfast alongside a whole-wheat bagel spread with cream cheese and plum jam.

1 SERVING

⅔ cup apple juice

1 ½ tablespoons honey

¾ cup diced plum

½ cup diced strawberries

½ cup diced banana

Place the apple juice, honey, plum, strawberries, and banana in a blender and mix on low speed until the mixture is blended. Continue mixing, gradually increasing the speed, until the mixture is smooth. Pour the smoothie into a glass and garnish with an Apple Chip (see page 192), if desired.

Calories	336.28	Protein	2.45 g
Calories from fat	14.56	Total fat	1.62 g
Carbohydrates	85.00 g	Fiber	5.79 g
Calcium	34.55 g	Iron	1.42 mg
Potassium	860.90 mg	Beta-carotene	287.72 mcg
Magnesium	44.31 mg	Vitamin C	67.29 mg

Stand by Your Mango

Tammy couldn't have said it better. This smoothie is for everyone who loves the richly sweet flavors of mangoes, apricots, and bananas.

1 SERVING

½ cup apricot nectar

1 ½ tablespoons honey

1 cup diced mango

½ cup diced apricots

½ cup diced banana

Place the apricot nectar, honey, mango, apricots, and banana in a blender and mix on low speed until the mixture is blended. Continue mixing, gradually increasing the speed, until the mixture is smooth. Pour the smoothie into a glass and garnish with a Fruit Skewer (see page 200), if desired.

Calories	382.75	Protein	3.33 g
Calories from fat	11.16	Total fat	1.24 g
Carbohydrates	99.04 g	Fiber	7.57 g
Calcium	43.24 g	Iron	1.50 mg
Potassium	958.20 mg	Beta-carotene	6159.31 mcg
Magnesium	50.11 mg	Vitamin C	61.69 mg

Ta-ta and Cherry-O

Whether you're a graduate of Cambridge or Oxford (or just a Beatles fan), you'll enjoy this Sterling smoothie. For a Buckingham Palace touch, serve with an assortment of scones.

1 SERVING

½ cup peach nectar

1 tablespoon honey

1 cup diced cherries

½ cup diced peach

Place the peach nectar, honey, cherries, and peach in a blender and mix on low speed until the mixture is blended. Continue mixing, gradually increasing the speed, until the mixture is smooth. Pour the smoothie into a glass and garnish with a Pineapple Bow (see page 206), if desired.

Calories	272.59	Protein	2.73 g
Calories from fat	13.44	Total fat	1.49 g
Carbohydrates	68.22 g	Fiber	5.82 g
Calcium	33.50 g	Iron	0.98 mg
Potassium	553.07 mg	Beta-carotene	550.77 mcg
Magnesium	27.30 mg	Vitamin C	22.46 mg

Te-kiwi Sunrise

This colorful and tasty smoothie looks just like its more potent namesake, but you won't find a worm floating at the bottom of your glass. Serve this colorful delight with friends while you lounge on the deck and be sure to have plenty of tortilla chips and salsa on hand.

1 SERVING

⅔ cup pineapple juice

1 ½ tablespoons honey

¾ cup diced kiwi

½ cup diced strawberries

½ cup diced banana

1 tablespoon grenadine syrup (optional)

Place the pineapple juice, honey, kiwi, strawberries, and banana in a blender and mix on low speed until the mixture is blended. Continue mixing, gradually increasing the speed, until the mixture is smooth. Pour the grenadine into a glass (optional) and add the smoothie. Garnish with a Pineapple Chip (see page 207), if desired.

Calories	358.16	Protein	2.69 g
Calories from fat	11.26	Total fat	1.25 g
Carbohydrates	89.34 g	Fiber	8.29 g
Calcium	52.54 g	Iron	1.23 mg
Potassium	1098.70 mg	Beta-carotene	254.82 mcg
Magnesium	70.51 mg	Vitamin C	224.14 mg

The Pear Rich Project

It's scary to think that you might run out of the necessary ingredients to create this frightfully delicious smoothie.

1 SERVING

⅔ cup pear nectar

1 tablespoon honey

1 cup diced pear

½ cup diced strawberries

Place the pear nectar, honey, pear, and strawberries in a blender and mix on low speed until the mixture is blended. Continue mixing, gradually increasing the speed, until the mixture is smooth. Pour the smoothie into a glass and garnish the rim with a Strawberry Fan (see page 215), if desired.

Calories	286.66	Protein	1.40 g
Calories from fat	8.85	Total fat	0.98 g
Carbohydrates	74.48 g	Fiber	6.91 g
Calcium	39.37 g	Iron	1.25 mg
Potassium	376.71 mg	Beta-carotene	34.25 mcg
Magnesium	23.62 mg	Vitamin C	55.60 mg

The Sleek-est Drink

Out of a possible 2,000 calories, this drink has only a meager 351. You don't know why? Good-bye.

1 SERVING

⅔ cup apricot nectar

1 ½ tablespoons honey

½ cup diced apricots

½ cup diced cherries

½ cup diced banana

Place the apricot nectar, honey, apricots, cherries, and banana in a blender and mix on low speed until the mixture is blended. Continue mixing, gradually increasing the speed, until the mixture is smooth. Pour the smoothie into a glass and garnish with a Fruit Skewer (see page 200), if desired.

Calories	351.12	Protein	3.51 g
Calories from fat	13.76	Total fat	1.53 g
Carbohydrates	89.01 g	Fiber	6.52 g
Calcium	40.55 g	Iron	1.73 mg
Potassium	910.89 mg	Beta-carotene	2721.47 mcg
Magnesium	45.33 mg	Vitamin C	21.31 mg

The Twist

Rev up the blender and do this cantaloupe, peach, and raspberry twist. It's a perfect touch for a nostalgia party. Don't forget to serve with a dish of peppermint sticks.

1 SERVING

½ cup apricot nectar

1 ½ tablespoons honey

½ cup raspberries

½ cup diced cantaloupe

½ cup diced peach

Place the apricot nectar, honey, raspberries, cantaloupe, and peach in a blender and mix on low speed until the mixture is blended. Continue mixing, gradually increasing the speed, until the mixture is smooth. Pour the smoothie into a glass and garnish with a Fruit Skewer (see page 200), if desired.

Calories	261.58	Protein	2.42 g
Calories from fat	6.77	Total fat	0.75 g
Carbohydrates	67.49 g	Fiber	7.34 g
Calcium	37.27 g	Iron	1.22 mg
Potassium	667.73 mg	Beta-carotene	2773.51 mcg
Magnesium	32.73 mg	Vitamin C	55.66 mg

War of the Whirls

No science fiction here. This sensational cherry, peach, and banana smoothie is truly out of this world. On this planet, serve it with a nutritious after-school snack.

1 SERVING

½ cup apple juice

1 ½ tablespoons honey

½ cup diced cherries

½ cup diced peach

½ cup diced banana

1 cup frozen mini orange-juice cubes

Place the apple juice, honey, cherries, peach, banana, and orange-juice cubes in a blender and mix on low speed until the mixture is blended. Continue mixing, gradually increasing the speed, until the mixture is smooth. Pour the smoothie into a glass and garnish with an Apple Chip (see page 192), if desired.

Calories	312.64	Protein	2.41 g
Calories from fat	11.42	Total fat	1.27 g
Carbohydrates	79.68 g	Fiber	5.36 g
Calcium	30.21 g	Iron	1.20 mg
Potassium	790.94 mg	Beta-carotene	346.38 mcg
Magnesium	40.03 mg	Vitamin C	18.78 mg

Moootown Smoothies

Dare-E to Be Different

For many of us, nothing is more refreshing and satisfying than a simple smoothie made with fruit juice and fruit. However, if you haven't yet sampled a smoothie made with milk or yogurt, you're in for a real treat because these dairy ingredients endow a smoothie with a creamier texture and a richer taste. Just as important, this combination of ingredients allows you to reap the health benefits of both fruit and dairy, each vital components of the food pyramid. Once you've enjoyed the smooth-as-silk taste of such creations as *Supermango, Blizzard of Oz,* or *Peach a' Cake,* you'll be eager to sample all 37 smoothie recipes in this chapter.

As you read through these recipes, you'll note that some of them call for using lowfat or fat-free ingredients. These are intended only as suggestions. Whole milk or regular yogurt works just as well if that suits your taste. If you're seeking more ways to add soybean products to your diet, try substituting tofu, soy milk, and soy yogurt for the dairy products suggested in these recipes (see chapter 6 for a host of suggestions on the use of soy products).

It's summertime, and the fruit is lusciously fresh and aromatic, so grab a healthful carton of your favorite grade A and head for the blender. You're on your way to becoming a smoothie digni-dairy.

Apple-Elation Trail

Peak enjoyment awaits you when you delight in the mountain of flavors found in this apple smoothie. Its tastes range from sweet apple to spicy cinnamon—one sip, and you'll agree it was worth the trek. True to its name, it's the ideal smoothie to share with friends after a long hike or a bike ride.

1 SERVING

½ cup apple juice

1 ½ tablespoons honey

1 ½ cups diced apple

¼ teaspoon ground cinnamon

¼ teaspoon ground nutmeg

½ cup vanilla fat-free frozen yogurt

Place the apple juice, honey, apple, cinnamon, nutmeg, and yogurt in a blender and mix on low speed until the mixture is blended. Continue mixing, gradually increasing the speed, until the mixture is smooth. Pour the smoothie into a glass and garnish with two Cinnamon-Coated Fusilli (see page 195), if desired.

Calories	370.11	Protein	4.58 g
Calories from fat	9.11	Total fat	1.01 g
Carbohydrates	90.93 g	Fiber	5.64 g
Calcium	129.85 g	Iron	1.49 mg
Potassium	571.64 mg	Beta-carotene	40.17 mcg
Magnesium	14.74 mg	Vitamin C	11.98 mg

Apricot and Raspberry Milk-Shrek

Don't be caught "dragon" your feet making this smoothie, or you'll be swamped with requests for this y-ogre-t delight.

1 SERVING

½ cup 2% milk

1 tablespoon honey

1 cup diced apricots

½ cup raspberries

½ cup raspberry lowfat frozen yogurt

Place the milk, honey, apricots, raspberries, and yogurt in a blender and mix on low speed until the mixture is blended. Continue mixing, gradually increasing the speed, until the mixture is smooth. Pour the smoothie into a glass and garnish with Berries on a Skewer (see page 194), if desired.

Calories	336.03	Protein	11.40 g
Calories from fat	41.63	Total fat	4.63 g
Carbohydrates	67.22 g	Fiber	8.18 g
Calcium	339.68 g	Iron	1.47 mg
Potassium	977.80 mg	Beta-carotene	2593.03 mcg
Magnesium	56.02 mg	Vitamin C	33.81 mg

Apropos Apricot

Because fresh apricots are so abundant in the sum-mertime, it's the most opportune time to enjoy this seasonably sensational apricot smoothie. After working all day in the garden, reward yourself with a glassful of this colorful fusion of apricots and bananas.

1 SERVING

½ cup apricot nectar

1 tablespoon honey

1 ¼ cups diced apricots

½ cup diced banana

½ cup vanilla lowfat yogurt

Place the apricot nectar, honey, apricots, banana, and yogurt in a blender and mix on low speed until the mixture is blended. Continue mixing, gradually increasing the speed, until the mixture is smooth. Pour the smoothie into a glass and garnish with a Crisp Banana Wafer (see page 198), if desired.

Calories	404.37	Protein	8.60 g
Calories from fat	23.21	Total fat	2.58 g
Carbohydrates	94.47 g	Fiber	7.55 g
Calcium	196.86 g	Iron	1.99 mg
Potassium	1258.12 mg	Beta-carotene	4235.00 mcg
Magnesium	59.60 mg	Vitamin C	28.98 mg

Banana Karenina

Count on it! You'll fall hopelessly in love with this novel USSR (Unbelievably Satisfying Smoothie Recipe), and you'll be "Russian" to have your friends over to share it.

1 SERVING

¼ cup apple juice

1 tablespoon honey

1 cup diced banana

½ cup vanilla lowfat yogurt

Place the apple juice, honey, banana, and yogurt in a blender and mix on low speed until the mixture is blended. Continue mixing, gradually increasing the speed, until the mixture is smooth. Pour the smoothie into a glass and garnish with a Crisp Banana Wafer (see page 198), if desired.

Calories	333.23	Protein	6.05 g
Calories from fat	18.81	Total fat	2.09 g
Carbohydrates	78.29 g	Fiber	3.70 g
Calcium	168.04 g	Iron	0.86 mg
Potassium	875.33 mg	Beta-carotene	72.25 mcg
Magnesium	60.43 mg	Vitamin C	14.09 mg

Berry, Berry Quite Contrary

How does this smoothie grow? No silver bells or cockle shells—just the wonderful tastes of fresh berries and yogurt with a dollop of honey.

1 SERVING

¼ cup apple juice

½ tablespoon honey

¾ cup diced banana

¼ cup blackberries

¼ cup blueberries

½ cup vanilla lowfat yogurt

Place the apple juice, honey, banana, blackberries, blueberries, and yogurt in a blender and mix on low speed until the mixture is blended. Continue mixing, gradually increasing the speed, until the mixture is smooth. Pour the smoothie into a glass and garnish with Berries on a Skewer (see page 194), if desired.

Calories	305.55	Protein	6.14 g
Calories from fat	19.69	Total fat	2.19 g
Carbohydrates	70.49 g	Fiber	5.67 g
Calcium	178.85 g	Iron	0.96 mg
Potassium	824.14 mg	Beta-carotene	93.28 mcg
Magnesium	58.36 mg	Vitamin C	23.79 mg

Berry-Go-Round

Don't worry if that brass ring is beyond your grasp—this deliciously sweet smoothie will delight you whether you are up or down. Complement the fresh taste of berries with a strawberry dipped in white chocolate.

1 SERVING

½ cup peach nectar

1 ½ tablespoons honey

1 cup diced strawberries

½ cup diced peach

½ cup peach lowfat frozen yogurt

Place the peach nectar, honey, strawberries, peach, and yogurt in a blender and mix on low speed until the mixture is blended. Continue mixing, gradually increasing the speed, until the mixture is smooth. Pour the smoothie into a glass and garnish the rim with a Strawberry Fan (see page 215), if desired.

Calories	351.88	Protein	6.45 g
Calories from fat	18.16	Total fat	2.02 g
Carbohydrates	83.05 g	Fiber	6.33 g
Calcium	189.05 g	Iron	1.17 mg
Potassium	705.87 mg	Beta-carotene	409.61 mcg
Magnesium	42.82 mg	Vitamin C	107.16 mg

Black-and-Blue

You'll be very sore-y if you don't give this blueberry and blackberry smoothie a fighting chance. It's truly a berry lover's dream.

1 SERVING

½ cup 2% milk

1 tablespoon honey

½ cup blackberries

½ cup blueberries

½ cup strawberry lowfat frozen yogurt

Place the milk, honey, blackberries, blueberries, and yogurt in a blender and mix on low speed until the mixture is blended. Continue mixing, gradually increasing the speed, until the mixture is smooth. Pour the smoothie into a glass and garnish with Berries on a Skewer (see page 194), if desired.

Calories	304.73	Protein	9.54 g
Calories from fat	37.80	Total fat	4.20 g
Carbohydrates	61.19 g	Fiber	5.82 g
Calcium	330.44 g	Iron	0.76 mg
Potassium	601.56 mg	Beta-carotene	78.06 mcg
Magnesium	49.78 mg	Vitamin C	26.48 mg

Blizzard of Oz

With just a little heart, courage, and a brain, you can start a blizzard in your kitchen. Just click your shoes; add the fruit, yogurt, and juice to the blender; and follow the mellow drink road.

1 SERVING

¼ cup apple juice

1 tablespoon honey

½ cup diced cherries

½ cup diced strawberries

½ cup raspberries

½ cup vanilla lowfat yogurt

Place the apple juice, honey, cherries, strawberries, raspberries, and yogurt in a blender and mix on low speed until the mixture is blended. Continue mixing, gradually increasing the speed, until the mixture is smooth. Pour the smoothie into a glass and garnish with an Apple Chip (see page 192), if desired.

Calories	302.47	Protein	6.44 g
Calories from fat	24.40	Total fat	2.71 g
Carbohydrates	68.08 g	Fiber	7.86 g
Calcium	195.06 g	Iron	1.34 mg
Potassium	674.99 mg	Beta-carotene	121.71 mcg
Magnesium	44.28 mg	Vitamin C	68.85 mg

Blueberry Chill

On sultry summer days, you'll definitely find a thrill with Blueberry Chill. You'll be equally delighted to find how easy it is to whip up a batch of this pleasingly sweet smoothie.

1 SERVING

½ cup peach nectar

1 tablespoon honey

1 cup blueberries

½ cup diced cherries

½ cup banana lowfat frozen yogurt

Place the peach nectar, honey, blueberries, cherries, and yogurt in a blender and mix on low speed until the mixture is blended. Continue mixing, gradually increasing the speed, until the mixture is smooth. Pour the smoothie into a glass and garnish with a Pineapple Bow (see page 206), if desired.

Calories	366.72	Protein	6.65 g
Calories from fat	23.16	Total fat	2.57 g
Carbohydrates	85.72 g	Fiber	6.37 g
Calcium	180.50 g	Iron	0.93 mg
Potassium	548.80 mg	Beta-carotene	327.90 mcg
Magnesium	35.28 mg	Vitamin C	31.30 mg

Blue Moon

If you indulge, once, in a blue moon, you'll be hooked on this blueberry, raspberry, and banana dairy treat.

1 SERVING

¹/₂ cup apple juice

2 tablespoons 2% milk

1 ¹/₂ tablespoons honey

1 cup blueberries

¹/₂ cup raspberries

¹/₂ cup diced banana

¹/₂ cup strawberry lowfat frozen yogurt

Place the apple juice, milk, honey, blueberries, raspberries, banana, and yogurt in a blender and mix on low speed until the mixture is blended. Continue mixing, gradually increasing the speed, until the mixture is smooth. Pour the smoothie into a glass and garnish with Berries on a Skewer (see page 194), if desired.

Calories	452.06	Protein	7.90 g
Calories from fat	29.46	Total fat	3.27 g
Carbohydrates	105.75 g	Fiber	10.08 g
Calcium	227.83 g	Iron	1.51 mg
Potassium	927.24 mg	Beta-carotene	147.49 mcg
Magnesium	63.25 mg	Vitamin C	43.29 mg

Cantaloupe? Need a Ladder!

Take a vow to wed the flavors of these glorious two fruits and enjoy them in richness and in health. Once your favorite container is filled with this flavorful concoction, you won't have to worry because "breaking cup is hard to do."

1 SERVING

¼ cup orange juice

1 ½ tablespoons honey

1 cup diced cantaloupe

½ cup diced banana

½ cup vanilla lowfat yogurt

½ cup frozen mini orange-juice cubes

Place the orange juice, honey, cantaloupe, banana, yogurt, and orange-juice cubes in a blender and mix on low speed until the mixture is blended. Continue mixing, gradually increasing the speed, until the mixture is smooth. Pour the smoothie into a glass and garnish the rim with an Orange Wheel (see page 202), if desired.

Calories	407.00	Protein	7.99 g
Calories from fat	22.34	Total fat	2.48 g
Carbohydrates	94.92 g	Fiber	3.52 g
Calcium	197.89 g	Iron	1.15 mg
Potassium	1376.46 mg	Beta-carotene	3177.19 mcg
Magnesium	75.10 mg	Vitamin C	168.18 mg

Cherry-Oke

You can't help being vocal about the harmony of flavors found in this note-able smoothie. Go ahead and see if you can cherry a tune. While you're at it, have a karaoke party and serve glassfuls of this flavorful delight.

1 SERVING

¼ cup apple juice

½ tablespoon honey

1 cup diced cherries

1 cup diced banana

½ cup vanilla lowfat yogurt

Place the apple juice, honey, cherries, banana, and yogurt in a blender and mix on low speed until the mixture is blended. Continue mixing, gradually increasing the speed, until the mixture is smooth. Pour the smoothie into a glass and garnish with a Pineapple Bow (see page 206), if desired.

Calories	405.43	Protein	7.76 g
Calories from fat	31.34	Total fat	3.48 g
Carbohydrates	93.56 g	Fiber	7.02 g
Calcium	189.15 g	Iron	1.38 mg
Potassium	1194.62 mg	Beta-carotene	240.31 mcg
Magnesium	76.17 mg	Vitamin C	25.08 mg

Goldilocks and the Three Berries

"Someone's been drinking my smoothie!" will be a common complaint by those not keeping an eye on their glassful of this irresistibly tempting strawberry, raspberry, and blueberry blend. Share it with friends and family, if you can bear it.

1 SERVING

⅓ cup apple juice

1½ tablespoons honey

½ cup diced strawberries

½ cup raspberries

½ cup diced banana

½ cup blueberry lowfat frozen yogurt

Place the apple juice, honey, strawberries, raspberries, banana, and yogurt in a blender and mix on low speed until the mixture is blended. Continue mixing, gradually increasing the speed, until the mixture is smooth. Pour the smoothie into a glass and garnish with Berries on a Skewer (see page 194), if desired.

Calories	361.19	Protein	6.39 g
Calories from fat	21.58	Total fat	2.40 g
Carbohydrates	84.80 g	Fiber	8.04 g
Calcium	190.77 g	Iron	1.41 mg
Potassium	839.69 mg	Beta-carotene	73.77 mcg
Magnesium	58.89 mg	Vitamin C	70.84 mg

In It for the Honey

No noble motives are necessary to make this deca-dently sweet smoothie. Just turn on the blender and enjoy! For added enjoyment, dunk a few honey graham crackers in this delicately flavored nectar.

1 SERVING

3 tablespoons 2% milk

¼ cup honey

1 cup diced banana

½ cup banana lowfat frozen yogurt

Place the milk, honey, banana, and yogurt in a blender and mix on low speed until the mixture is blended. Continue mixing, gradually increasing the speed, until the mixture is smooth. Pour the smoothie into a glass and garnish with a Crisp Banana Wafer (see page 198), if desired.

Calories	520.05	Protein	7.73 g
Calories from fat	26.10	Total fat	2.90 g
Carbohydrates	125.62 g	Fiber	3.77 g
Calcium	223.14 g	Iron	0.92 mg
Potassium	905.24 mg	Beta-carotene	72.00 mcg
Magnesium	66.10 mg	Vitamin C	15.18 mg

I Peel Good...
Like I Knew I Would

The taste of this delightfully tangy orange smoothie can only be described in the immortal words of the Godfather of Soul—"Whoa-oa-oa-oa!"

1 SERVING

2 tablespoons orange juice

1 tablespoon honey

¾ cup diced orange

¾ cup diced banana

1 cup frozen mini orange juice cubes

½ cup vanilla lowfat yogurt

Place the orange juice, honey, orange, banana, orange-juice cubes, and yogurt in a blender and mix on low speed until the mixture is blended. Continue mixing, gradually increasing the speed, until the mixture is smooth. Pour the smoothie into a glass and garnish the rim with an Orange Wheel (see page 202), if desired.

Calories	452.07	Protein	8.86 g
Calories from fat	22.60	Total fat	2.51 g
Carbohydrates	105.67 g	Fiber	6.27 g
Calcium	241.64 g	Iron	1.22 mg
Potassium	1431.32 mg	Beta-carotene	199.24 mcg
Magnesium	90.76 mg	Vitamin C	221.42 mg

Lime Dancing

Take two steps forward and deposit some lime-juice cubes in your blender. You've just learned lime dancing. Now, step back and enjoy this deliciously tangy lime smoothie.

1 SERVING

⅔ cup orange juice

1½ tablespoons honey

¾ cup diced banana

½ cup diced strawberries

½ cup vanilla fat-free frozen yogurt

⅓ cup mini frozen lime-juice cubes

Place the orange juice, honey, banana, strawberries, yogurt, and lime-juice cubes in a blender and mix on low speed until the mixture is blended. Continue mixing, gradually increasing the speed, until the mixture is smooth. Pour the smoothie into a glass and garnish the rim with a Lime Wheel (see page 202), if desired.

Calories	421.55	Protein	7.28 g
Calories from fat	11.34	Total fat	1.26 g
Carbohydrates	103.96 g	Fiber	5.33 g
Calcium	145.84 g	Iron	1.65 mg
Potassium	1209.85 mg	Beta-carotene	133.46 mcg
Magnesium	64.67 mg	Vitamin C	164.15 mg

Lord of the Bings

This cherry delight should be the most popular form of refreshment in Middle-Earth and will be in your home, too. Offer this flavorful refreshment to friends and family any time of the year.

1 SERVING

½ cup apricot nectar

1 ½ tablespoons honey

1 cup diced cherries

½ cup diced strawberries

½ cup raspberry lowfat frozen yogurt

Place the apricot nectar, honey, cherries, strawberries, and yogurt in a blender and mix on low speed until the mixture is blended. Continue mixing, gradually increasing the speed, until the mixture is smooth. Pour the smoothie into a glass and garnish with a Pineapple Bow (see page 206), if desired.

Calories	397.88	Protein	7.21 g
Calories from fat	28.02	Total fat	3.11 g
Carbohydrates	92.51 g	Fiber	6.06 g
Calcium	197.49 g	Iron	1.57 mg
Potassium	818.71 mg	Beta-carotene	1169.19 mcg
Magnesium	45.81 mg	Vitamin C	58.79 mg

Material Swirl

Nothing can possibly make you Mad-onna day you taste this cinnamon-rich combination of fruits and honey.

1 SERVING

¾ cup 2% milk

1 tablespoon honey

½ cup blueberries

½ cup diced peach

½ cup diced banana

¼ teaspoon ground cinnamon

Place the milk, honey, blueberries, peach, banana, and cinnamon in a blender and mix on low speed until the mixture is blended. Continue mixing, gradually increasing the speed, until the mixture is smooth. Pour the smoothie into a glass and garnish with a Fruit Skewer (see page 200), if desired.

Calories	303.16	Protein	8.04 g
Calories from fat	38.04	Total fat	4.23 g
Carbohydrates	63.89 g	Fiber	5.78 g
Calcium	242.02 g	Iron	0.67 mg
Potassium	822.54 mg	Beta-carotene	306.42 mcg
Magnesium	56.76 mg	Vitamin C	23.71 mg

Moo'd Indigo

The only thing blue about this upbeat smoothie is its color. So share the joy with good friends at a TGIF get-together.

1 SERVING

⅓ cup apple juice

1 ½ tablespoons honey

1 cup blueberries

½ cup diced banana

½ cup blueberry lowfat frozen yogurt

Place the apple juice, honey, blueberries, banana, and yogurt in a blender and mix on low speed until the mixture is blended. Continue mixing, gradually increasing the speed, until the mixture is smooth. Pour the smoothie into a glass and garnish with an Apple Chip (see page 192), if desired.

Calories	387.35	Protein	6.30 g
Calories from fat	20.73	Total fat	2.30 g
Carbohydrates	92.35 g	Fiber	5.86 g
Calcium	174.32 g	Iron	0.99 mg
Potassium	737.48 mg	Beta-carotene	123.34 mcg
Magnesium	46.77 mg	Vitamin C	27.25 mg

Peach a' Cake

Ask any New York cabbie how easy it is to prepare this deliciously refreshing smoothie.

1 SERVING

¼ cup apple juice

1 tablespoon honey

1 cup diced peach

½ cup diced banana

½ cup vanilla lowfat yogurt

Place the apple juice, honey, peach, banana, and yogurt in a blender and mix on low speed until the mixture is blended. Continue mixing, gradually increasing the speed, until the mixture is smooth. Pour the smoothie into a glass and garnish with a Fruit Skewer (see page 200), if desired.

Calories	337.33	Protein	6.47 g
Calories from fat	16.95	Total fat	1.88 g
Carbohydrates	79.59 g	Fiber	5.30 g
Calcium	172.04 g	Iron	0.81 mg
Potassium	913.23 mg	Beta-carotene	487.94 mcg
Magnesium	50.58 mg	Vitamin C	19.38 mg

Pineapple Twist

Add some pineapple and mango to a blender and watch it go round and round and up and down. Next, show your friends—you drink the twist like this.

1 SERVING

½ cup peach nectar

1 ½ tablespoons honey

1 cup diced pineapple

½ cup diced mango

½ cup peach lowfat frozen yogurt

Place the peach nectar, honey, pineapple, mango, and yogurt in a blender and mix on low speed until the mixture is blended. Continue mixing, gradually increasing the speed, until the mixture is smooth. Pour the smoothie into a glass and garnish with a Pineapple Wedge (see page 209), if desired.

Calories	395.10	Protein	5.86 g
Calories from fat	19.94	Total fat	2.22 g
Carbohydrates	95.19 g	Fiber	4.16 g
Calcium	180.66 g	Iron	1.13 mg
Potassium	566.71 mg	Beta-carotene	2100.55 mcg
Magnesium	49.39 mg	Vitamin C	54.15 mg

Rasmanian Devil

This raspberry smoothie is one mean drink. Even if you are not from Down Under, you'll keep coming back for more. To add interest to your breakfast fare, spoon some of this smoothie over a Belgian waffle and top with fresh raspberries.

1 SERVING

½ cup 2% milk

1 tablespoon honey

1 cup raspberries

½ cup diced banana

½ cup vanilla lowfat yogurt

Place the milk, honey, raspberries, banana, and yogurt in a blender and mix on low speed until the mixture is blended. Continue mixing, gradually increasing the speed, until the mixture is smooth. Pour the smoothie into a glass and garnish with Berries on a Skewer (see page 194), if desired.

Calories	355.96	Protein	10.43 g
Calories from fat	42.13	Total fat	4.68 g
Carbohydrates	73.56 g	Fiber	10.21 g
Calcium	334.61 g	Iron	1.16 mg
Potassium	879.88 mg	Beta-carotene	83.97 mcg
Magnesium	75.64 mg	Vitamin C	39.51 mg

Roller Coaster Ki-Whee

Fasten your seat belt, hold on tight, and get ready for this thrill in a glass. Make a batch, and you'll agree, it's a screaming success.

1 SERVING

²⁄₃ cup peach nectar

1 ½ tablespoons honey

¾ cup diced kiwi

½ cup diced banana

½ cup peach lowfat frozen yogurt

Place the peach nectar, honey, kiwi, banana, and yogurt in a blender and mix on low speed until the mixture is blended. Continue mixing, gradually increasing the speed, until the mixture is smooth. Pour the smoothie into a glass and garnish with a Fruit Skewer (see page 200), if desired.

Calories	437.91	Protein	7.04 g
Calories from fat	20.51	Total fat	2.28 g
Carbohydrates	105.06 g	Fiber	7.37 g
Calcium	202.65 g	Iron	1.30 mg
Potassium	1017.19 mg	Beta-carotene	388.53 mcg
Magnesium	83.50 mg	Vitamin C	146.55 mg

Santana Banana

To deserve a taste of this enticing banana and peach smoothie, even a black magic woman would change her evil ways.

1 SERVING

½ cup peach nectar

1 tablespoon honey

1 cup diced banana

½ cup diced peach

½ cup vanilla lowfat yogurt

Place the peach nectar, honey, banana, peach, and yogurt in a blender and mix on low speed until the mixture is blended. Continue mixing, gradually increasing the speed, until the mixture is smooth. Pour the smoothie into a glass and garnish with a sprig of fresh mint (see page 205), if desired.

Calories	407.87	Protein	6.95 g
Calories from fat	19.11	Total fat	2.12 g
Carbohydrates	97.81 g	Fiber	6.09 g
Calcium	174.17 g	Iron	0.96 mg
Potassium	1018.80 mg	Beta-carotene	454.71 mcg
Magnesium	69.50 mg	Vitamin C	26.64 mg

Scary Smoothie #3

This fruit-filled smoothie is so delicious, it's frightening. It definitely has no s-equal. Serve this wonderful five-fruit medley the next time you get together to watch movies with family or friends.

1 SERVING

⅓ cup apple juice

1 tablespoon honey

½ cup diced nectarine

½ cup diced banana

½ cup blueberries

½ cup peach lowfat frozen yogurt

Place the apple juice, honey, nectarine, banana, blueberries, and yogurt in a blender and mix on low speed until the mixture is blended. Continue mixing, gradually increasing the speed, until the mixture is smooth. Pour the smoothie into a glass and garnish with an Apple Chip (see page 192), if desired.

Calories	348.36	Protein	6.43 g
Calories from fat	21.11	Total fat	2.35 g
Carbohydrates	81.50 g	Fiber	4.99 g
Calcium	172.78 g	Iron	0.93 mg
Potassium	813.73 mg	Beta-carotene	333.07 mcg
Magnesium	48.45 mg	Vitamin C	21.50 mg

Shake Your Fruity

*Turn up the volume and shake, shake, shake . . .
shake, shake, shake . . . shake your fruity smoothie.
Try this fruit-filled delight when you're looking for
some excitement during your next coffee break.*

1 SERVING

½ cup 2% milk

2 tablespoons peach nectar

1½ tablespoons honey

1 cup blueberries

½ cup diced cherries

½ cup blueberry lowfat frozen yogurt

Place the milk, peach nectar, honey, blueberries,
cherries, and yogurt in a blender and mix on low
speed until the mixture is blended. Continue
mixing, gradually increasing the speed, until the
mixture is smooth. Pour the smoothie into a
glass and garnish with Berries on a Skewer (see
page 194), if desired.

Calories	409.10	Protein	10.49 g
Calories from fat	44.08	Total fat	4.90 g
Carbohydrates	87.31 g	Fiber	5.83 g
Calcium	324.82 g	Iron	0.86 mg
Potassium	705.33 mg	Beta-carotene	210.25 mcg
Magnesium	48.43 mg	Vitamin C	27.56 mg

Splendor in the Glass

One glimpse of the deep-golden appearance of this rich pineapple smoothie, and it will be love at first sight.

1 SERVING

½ cup 2% milk

2 tablespoons apricot nectar

1 ½ tablespoons honey

1 cup diced pineapple

½ cup diced banana

½ cup pineapple lowfat frozen yogurt

Place the milk, apricot nectar, honey, pineapple, banana, and yogurt in a blender and mix on low speed until the mixture is blended. Continue mixing, gradually increasing the speed, until the mixture is smooth. Pour the smoothie into a glass and garnish the rim with a Pineapple Slice (see page 209), if desired.

Calories	421.42	Protein	10.06 g
Calories from fat	42.29	Total fat	4.70 g
Carbohydrates	91.78 g	Fiber	3.91 g
Calcium	321.23 g	Iron	1.19 mg
Potassium	909.34 mg	Beta-carotene	301.06 mcg
Magnesium	76.98 mg	Vitamin C	32.87 mg

Summer in Pear-adise

Wouldn't it be nice if we could bring back all the summer days? This delightful pear and peach smoothie will make it seem like July in December. It's just as welcome at the beach as it is après-ski.

1 SERVING

⅔ cup peach nectar

1½ tablespoons honey

1 cup diced pear

½ cup diced peach

½ cup peach lowfat frozen yogurt

Place the peach nectar, honey, pear, peach, and yogurt in a blender and mix on low speed until the mixture is blended. Continue mixing, gradually increasing the speed, until the mixture is smooth. Pour the smoothie into a glass and garnish with a Fruit Skewer (see page 200), if desired.

Calories	421.84	Protein	6.19 g
Calories from fat	18.64	Total fat	2.07 g
Carbohydrates	102.10 g	Fiber	6.72 g
Calcium	186.03 g	Iron	1.03 mg
Potassium	653.16 mg	Beta-carotene	454.80 mcg
Magnesium	37.78 mg	Vitamin C	21.84 mg

Summerlime, Summerlime . . . Sum, Sum, Summerlime

One taste of this deliciously tangy apple, peach, and lime masterpiece, and you'll agree it's super-fine, superfine . . . sup, sup, superfine.

1 SERVING

½ cup apple juice

1 ½ tablespoons honey

1 cup diced peach

½ cup diced banana

1 carton (6 ounces) custard-style key lime pie yogurt

½ cup frozen mini lime-juice cubes

Place the apple juice, honey, peach, banana, yogurt, and lime-juice cubes in a blender and mix on low speed until the mixture is blended. Continue mixing, gradually increasing the speed, until the mixture is smooth. Pour the smoothie into a glass and garnish the rim with a Lime Wheel (see page 202), if desired.

Calories	510.20	Protein	9.67 g
Calories from fat	42.95	Total fat	4.77 g
Carbohydrates	118.20 g	Fiber	5.88 g
Calcium	284.66 g	Iron	1.05 mg
Potassium	1220.06 mg	Beta-carotene	494.96 mcg
Magnesium	45.39 mg	Vitamin C	55.36 mg

Summer Peach Party

Put on your shades, turn up the radio, and catch some rays, but keep cool with this intensely rich peach- and banana-flavored smoothie. Just fill a thermos with this refreshing blend before you head for the shore.

1 SERVING

⅓ cup apple juice

1 ½ tablespoons honey

1 cup diced peach

½ cup diced banana

½ cup peach lowfat frozen yogurt

Place the apple juice, honey, peach, banana, and yogurt in a blender and mix on low speed until the mixture is blended. Continue mixing, gradually increasing the speed, until the mixture is smooth. Pour the smoothie into a glass and garnish with an Apple Chip (see page 192), if desired.

Calories	379.25	Protein	6.52 g
Calories from fat	17.15	Total fat	1.91 g
Carbohydrates	90.73 g	Fiber	5.35 g
Calcium	174.12 g	. Iron	0.93 mg
Potassium	943.33 mg	Beta-carotene	488.03 mcg
Magnesium	51.42 mg	Vitamin C	19.62 mg

Supermango

Faster than a whirring blender, able to keep build-
ing in a single mound—it's Supermango.

1 SERVING

½ cup peach nectar

1 tablespoon honey

1 cup diced banana

½ cup diced mango

½ cup vanilla lowfat frozen yogurt

Place the peach nectar, honey, banana, mango,
and yogurt in a blender and mix on low speed
until the mixture is blended. Continue mixing,
gradually increasing the speed, until the mixture
is smooth. Pour the smoothie into a glass and
garnish with a sprig of fresh mint (see page 205),
if desired.

Calories	424.95	Protein	6.77 g
Calories from fat	20.42	Total fat	2.27 g
Carbohydrates	102.40 g	Fiber	5.87 g
Calcium	178.17 g	Iron	0.97 mg
Potassium	980.05 mg	Beta-carotene	2154.42 mcg
Magnesium	70.98 mg	Vitamin C	43.88 mg

Thank Heaven for Little Whirls

When your family quickly polishes off your first batch of this delightful nectarine smoothie, they can take comfort in the knowledge that little whirls get bigger every day.

1 SERVING

2 tablespoons apple juice

1 tablespoon honey

¾ cup diced nectarine

½ cup vanilla lowfat yogurt

½ cup frozen mini orange-juice cubes

Place the apple juice, honey, nectarine, yogurt, and orange-juice cubes in a blender and mix on low speed until the mixture is blended. Continue mixing, gradually increasing the speed, until the mixture is smooth. Pour the smoothie into a glass and garnish with an Apple Chip (see page 192), if desired.

Calories	295.50	Protein	6.92 g
Calories from fat	20.32	Total fat	2.26 g
Carbohydrates	65.17 g	Fiber	1.98 g
Calcium	197.26 g	Iron	0.61 mg
Potassium	755.33 mg	Beta-carotene	426.10 mcg
Magnesium	23.27 mg	Vitamin C	67.97 mg

Thanks a Melon

Serve this refreshingly light smoothie to friends on a hot summer day and sit back and wait for a chorus of "thanks a melon."

1 SERVING

¼ cup apple juice

1 tablespoon honey

1 cup diced cantaloupe

½ cup diced banana

½ cup vanilla lowfat yogurt

½ cup frozen mini orange-juice cubes

Place the apple juice, honey, cantaloupe, banana, yogurt, and orange-juice cubes in a blender and mix on low speed until the mixture is blended. Continue mixing, gradually increasing the speed, until the mixture is smooth. Pour the smoothie into a glass and garnish with a Fruit Skewer (see page 200), if desired.

Calories	384.85	Protein	8.15 g
Calories from fat	23.62	Total fat	2.62 g
Carbohydrates	87.54 g	Fiber	3.43 g
Calcium	216.35 g	Iron	1.13 mg
Potassium	1364.20 mg	Beta-carotene	3154.38 mcg
Magnesium	55.27 mg	Vitamin C	137.01 mg

The Trouble with Cherry

Goood Even-ing. Don't trouble yourself trying to figure out why this smoothie keeps mysteriously disappearing. It's quite obvious—it's delicious.

1 SERVING

⅔ cup peach nectar

1½ tablespoons honey

1½ cups diced cherries

½ cup vanilla lowfat frozen yogurt

Place the peach nectar, honey, cherries, and yogurt in a blender and mix on low speed until the mixture is blended. Continue mixing, gradually increasing the speed, until the mixture is smooth. Pour the smoothie into a glass and garnish with a Pineapple Bow (see page 206), if desired.

Calories	444.54	Protein	7.56 g
Calories from fat	30.81	Total fat	3.42 g
Carbohydrates	103.73 g	Fiber	6.06 g
Calcium	196.26 g	Iron	1.37 mg
Potassium	766.66 mg	Beta-carotene	461.24 mcg
Magnesium	45.85 mg	Vitamin C	24.85 mg

Tooth Berry

Because this smoothie is filled with berries and bananas, you may find this one filling. And if you don't brush your teeth, you'll probably need a drilling!

1 SERVING

¹⁄₃ cup 2% milk

1 tablespoon honey

¹⁄₂ cup blackberries

¹⁄₂ cup strawberries

¹⁄₂ cup diced banana

¹⁄₂ cup vanilla lowfat yogurt

¹⁄₂ cup frozen mini orange-juice cubes

Place the milk, honey, blackberries, strawberries, banana, yogurt, and orange-juice cubes in a blender and mix on low speed until the mixture is blended. Continue mixing, gradually increasing the speed, until the mixture is smooth. Pour the smoothie into a glass and garnish with Berries on a Skewer (see page 194), if desired.

Calories	401.95	Protein	10.44 g
Calories from fat	38.32	Total fat	4.26 g
Carbohydrates	85.84 g	Fiber	7.82 g
Calcium	327.97 g	Iron	1.34 mg
Potassium	1200.50 mg	Beta-carotene	130.13 mcg
Magnesium	69.63 mg	Vitamin C	131.88 mg

Two Plums Up

I'm sure even Roger would agree that this tasteful production, dripping with sweetness, is a gigantic summer hit. Rent some movies, gather around the TV, and serve this award-winning delight.

1 SERVING

⅔ cup apricot nectar

1 ½ tablespoons honey

1 cup diced plum

½ cup diced banana

½ cup strawberry lowfat frozen yogurt

Place the apricot nectar, honey, plum, banana, and yogurt in a blender and mix on low speed until the mixture is blended. Continue mixing, gradually increasing the speed, until the mixture is smooth. Pour the smoothie into a glass and garnish the rim with a Strawberry Fan (see page 215), if desired.

Calories	451.75	Protein	7.20 g
Calories from fat	25.52	Total fat	2.84 g
Carbohydrates	107.75 g	Fiber	5.34 g
Calcium	178.15 g	Iron	1.24 mg
Potassium	984.62 mg	Beta-carotene	1669.71 mcg
Magnesium	56.95 mg	Vitamin C	24.33 mg

Yogi Berry

As Yogi would say, if people won't share this delightfully rich blueberry smoothie with you, you can't stop 'em.

1 SERVING

¼ cup pineapple juice

½ tablespoon honey

1 cup blueberries

½ cup vanilla lowfat yogurt

Place the pineapple juice, honey, blueberries, and yogurt in a blender and mix on low speed until the mixture is blended. Continue mixing, gradually increasing the speed, until the mixture is smooth. Pour the smoothie into a glass and garnish with Berries on a Skewer (see page 194), if desired.

Calories	255.91	Protein	6.00 g
Calories from fat	18.46	Total fat	2.05 g
Carbohydrates	55.72 g	Fiber	3.94 g
Calcium	184.34 g	Iron	0.29 mg
Potassium	452.06 mg	Beta-carotene	110.25 mcg
Magnesium	7.46 mg	Vitamin C	33.90 mg

CHAPTER 6

Smoothie Power

Fit and Trim, Filled to the Rim

Smoothies have become the rage among health-conscious individuals. Many of us who have grown up worshiping milk shakes, malts, and blizzards as the ultimate sweet temptation have come to realize that smoothies provide a delicious, guilt-free, healthy alternative. These flavorful concoctions are rich in vitamin C because of the wide variety of fruit they contain, and they can be an important source of protein and calcium when dairy products are added. However, as healthful as smoothies can be, they shouldn't be considered a meal replacement but rather enjoyed as a nutritious snack or a supplement to a meal. On the other hand, when you would like to transform a smoothie into an instant meal, there are a number of nutritional additives, breakfast powders, or protein supplements that can be added to achieve this goal. Just as the mealworthiness can be improved, the health benefits of smoothies can also be enhanced by the simple addition of one or more supplements, such as herbs or extracts. In chapter 1, I discuss several of these health-promoting boosters that have the potential to provide a variety of benefits, such as enhanced energy, improved memory, protection against colds, and relief from stress.

I have also discovered how to transform a smoothie into a healthier offering by preparing it with one or more soybean products, such as soy milk, tofu, or soy yogurt. What's amazing is that these soy ingredients are not only good for you, they add flavor to a smoothie as well.

In this chapter, you'll be pleased to discover 30 recipes that were designed to appeal to the most health-conscious among us. Some of my favorites are *If I Only Had a Bran, The Glass Is Always Greener,* and *A Bundle of Soy.* No matter which smoothie recipes turn out to be your favorites, you'll experience the satisfaction of knowing that with every sip, you're doing something good for yourself.

A Bundle of Soy

You'll be extremely pleased with this new arrival on your menu—and it doesn't require much labor. Celebrate any happy occasion by serving glassfuls of this healthful potion.

1 SERVING

½ cup pineapple juice

1 ½ tablespoons honey

½ teaspoon vanilla extract

1 cup diced banana

½ cup diced pineapple

½ cup diced mango

½ cup soft silken tofu

Place the pineapple juice, honey, vanilla, banana, pineapple, mango, and tofu in a blender and mix on low speed until the mixture is blended. Continue mixing, gradually increasing the speed, until the mixture is smooth. Pour the smoothie into a glass and garnish with a Pineapple Chip (see page 207), if desired.

Calories	459.83	Protein	7.81 g
Calories from fat	39.05	Total fat	4.34 g
Carbohydrates	103.52 g	Fiber	6.19 g
Calcium	59.97 g	Iron	1.92 mg
Potassium	1189.13 mg	Beta-carotene	2053.12 mcg
Magnesium	95.56 mg	Vitamin C	78.60 mg

A-Buzz and Beyond

This bee pollen–enriched masterpiece provides a new level of health and energy-boosting benefits for smoothie lovers. Enjoy this tonic before or after a workout.

1 SERVING

⅔ cup pineapple juice

1 tablespoon honey

¾ cup diced cantaloupe

½ cup diced pineapple

½ cup diced banana

½ cup pineapple lowfat frozen yogurt

1 tablespoon bee pollen, or according to specific-brand label recommendations

Place the pineapple juice, honey, cantaloupe, pineapple, banana, yogurt, and bee pollen in a blender and mix on low speed until the mixture is blended. Continue mixing, gradually increasing the speed, until the mixture is smooth. Pour the smoothie into a glass and garnish with a Pineapple Bow (see page 206), if desired.

Calories	401.73	Protein	6.60 g
Calories from fat	20.98	Total fat	2.33 g
Carbohydrates	93.11 g	Fiber	3.73 g
Calcium	177.82 g	Iron	0.93 mg
Potassium	1169.59 mg	Beta-carotene	2411.07 mcg
Magnesium	60.87 mg	Vitamin C	110.18 mg

Berry Bonds

Try this record-breaking berry, tofu, and protein smoothie. One sip, and you'll agree, it could be, it might be, it is—out of this world!

1 SERVING

½ cup vanilla-flavored Rice Dream

2 tablespoons orange juice

2 tablespoons honey

½ cup blackberries

½ cup blueberries

½ cup raspberries

½ cup soft silken tofu

1 tablespoon vanilla-flavored whey protein powder or favorite protein powder

Place the Rice Dream, orange juice, honey, blackberries, blueberries, raspberries, tofu, and protein powder in a blender and mix on low speed until the mixture is blended. Continue mixing, gradually increasing the speed, until the mixture is smooth. Pour the smoothie into a glass and garnish with Berries on a Skewer (see page 194), if desired.

Calories	488.51	Protein	12.06 g
Calories from fat	93.65	Total fat	10.41 g
Carbohydrates	92.14 g	Fiber	11.22 g
Calcium	102.03 g	Iron	2.77 mg
Potassium	647.28 mg	Beta-carotene	113.58 mcg
Magnesium	66.24 mg	Vitamin C	56.83 mg

Bran Prix

This high-performance banana and peach smoothie will get you off to a winning start each morning! For a complete, fiber-rich breakfast, serve with bran waffles or muffins.

1 SERVING

2 tablespoons orange juice

2 tablespoons 2% milk

1 tablespoon honey

1 cup diced banana

½ cup diced peach

½ cup vanilla fat-free yogurt

1 tablespoon wheat bran

Place the orange juice, milk, honey, banana, peach, yogurt, and bran in a blender and mix on low speed until the mixture is blended. Continue mixing, gradually increasing the speed, until the mixture is smooth. Pour the smoothie into a glass and garnish with a Fruit Skewer (see page 200), if desired.

Calories	375.89	Protein	8.00 g
Calories from fat	14.38	Total fat	1.60 g
Carbohydrates	90.06 g	Fiber	6.96 g
Calcium	157.67 g	Iron	1.61 mg
Potassium	1114.41 mg	Beta-carotene	309.38 mcg
Magnesium	79.60 mg	Vitamin C	35.16 mg

Cold Busters

Who you gonna call when you have a cold? Call for someone to make this smoothie, packed with orange juice and strawberries, supplemented with a generous dose of vitamin C.

1 SERVING

½ cup orange juice

1 ½ tablespoons honey

1 cup diced strawberries

½ cup diced peach

½ cup diced banana

½ cup strawberry lowfat frozen yogurt

Ginkgo biloba, according to specific-brand label
    recommendations

Ginseng, according to specific-brand label
    recommendations

1 tablespoon vitamin C, or according to specific-
    brand label recommendations

(continues)

Place the orange juice, honey, strawberries, peach, banana, yogurt, ginkgo, ginseng, and vitamin C in a blender and mix on low speed until the mixture is blended. Continue mixing, gradually increasing the speed, until the mixture is smooth. Pour the smoothie into a glass and garnish the rim with a Strawberry Fan (see page 215), if desired.

Calories	384.55	Protein	7.25 g
Calories from fat	20.64	Total fat	2.29 g
Carbohydrates	90.36 g	Fiber	5.72 g
Calcium	189.34 g	Iron	1.10 mg
Potassium	1063.29 mg	Beta-carotene	321.42 mcg
Magnesium	64.93 mg	Vitamin C	122.33 mg

FiberActive

Start the morning with a glassful of this protein, granola, and fruit smoothie. It's a classic example of ADHD (Absolutely Delicious and Healthful Drink).

1 SERVING

½ cup vanilla-flavored soy milk

1½ tablespoons honey

½ cup blackberries

½ cup diced apricots

½ cup diced banana

¼ cup granola

1 tablespoon vanilla-flavored whey protein powder

1 tablespoon wheat bran (optional)

Place the soy milk, honey, blackberries, apricots, banana, granola, protein powder, and bran (optional) in a blender and mix on low speed until the mixture is blended. Continue mixing, gradually increasing the speed, until the mixture is smooth. Pour the smoothie into a glass and garnish with Berries on a Skewer (see page 194), if desired.

Calories	469.05	Protein	13.23 g
Calories from fat	74.66	Total fat	8.30 g
Carbohydrates	92.72 g	Fiber	9.47 g
Calcium	81.86 g	Iron	2.99 mg
Potassium	920.54 mg	Beta-carotene	1355.08 mcg
Magnesium	89.90 mg	Vitamin C	30.35 mg

Flax or Fiction

Trust me, this is no urban legend. Made with melon, strawberry, and flax, this smoothie is rich in health-promoting omega-3 fatty acids.

1 SERVING

¼ cup peach nectar

¼ cup vanilla-flavored soy milk

2 tablespoons honey

1 cup diced cantaloupe

½ cup diced strawberries

½ cup soft silken tofu

Flaxseed oil, according to specific-brand label
   recommendations

Place the peach nectar, soy milk, honey, cantaloupe, strawberries, tofu, and flaxseed oil in a blender and mix on low speed until the mixture is blended. Continue mixing, gradually increasing the speed, until the mixture is smooth. Pour the smoothie into a glass and garnish the rim with a Strawberry Fan (see page 215), if desired.

Calories	342.60	Protein	9.37 g
Calories from fat	43.32	Total fat	4.81 g
Carbohydrates	71.48 g	Fiber	3.76 g
Calcium	79.87 g	Iron	2.32 mg
Potassium	947.19 mg	Beta-carotene	3163.88 mcg
Magnesium	71.96 mg	Vitamin C	118.09 mg

Fruitilicious

Are you ready to taste a smoothie that is too fruity for ya? Fill your glass or thermos with this wheat germ, soy milk, and fruit medley—it's destined to become a favorite healthful snack.

1 SERVING

¼ cup vanilla-flavored soy milk

2 tablespoons orange juice

1 ½ tablespoons honey

½ cup raspberries

½ cup blueberries

½ cup diced strawberries

½ cup diced banana

½ cup soft silken tofu

2 tablespoons wheat germ

Place the soy milk, orange juice, honey, raspberries, blueberries, strawberries, banana, tofu, and wheat germ in a blender and mix on low speed until the mixture is blended. Continue mixing, gradually increasing the speed, until the mixture is smooth. Pour the smoothie into a glass and garnish with Berries on a Skewer (see page 194), if desired.

Calories	426.22	Protein	13.13 g
Calories from fat	61.07	Total fat	6.79 g
Carbohydrates	86.32 g	Fiber	11.98 g
Calcium	89.92 g	Iron	3.49 mg
Potassium	1067.61 mg	Beta-carotene	128.46 mcg
Magnesium	125.87 mg	Vitamin C	94.34 mg

Fruity and the Yeast

Don't be alarmed if you fall in love with this surprising smoothie. With its healthful combination of mango, pineapple, and yeast, it's bound to become a favorite in your castle.

1 SERVING

¼ cup orange juice

1 ½ tablespoons honey

1 cup diced mango

½ cup diced pineapple

½ cup vanilla soy yogurt

1 tablespoon brewer's yeast, or according to specific-brand label recommendations

Place the orange juice, honey, mango, pineapple, yogurt, and yeast in a blender and mix on low speed until the mixture is blended. Continue mixing, gradually increasing the speed, until the mixture is smooth. Pour the smoothie into a glass and garnish with a Pineapple Spear (see page 209), if desired.

Calories	343.07	Protein	5.67 g
Calories from fat	20.12	Total fat	2.24 g
Carbohydrates	81.62 g	Fiber	4.09 g
Calcium	197.32 g	Iron	1.72 mg
Potassium	485.50 mg	Beta-carotene	3883.23 mcg
Magnesium	33.16 mg	Vitamin C	89.60 mg

Ginkgo, Ginkgo Little Star

You won't have a hard time remembering this rhyme once you make this ginkgo-enriched smoothie part of your daily diet. How you'll wonder why you didn't try it sooner.

1 SERVING

⅔ cup mango nectar

1 tablespoon honey

¾ cup diced kiwi

½ cup diced mango

½ cup diced banana

½ cup banana lowfat frozen yogurt

Ginkgo biloba, according to specific-brand label recommendations

Place the mango nectar, honey, kiwi, mango, banana, yogurt, and ginkgo in a blender and mix on low speed until the mixture is blended. Continue mixing, gradually increasing the speed, until the mixture is smooth. Pour the smoothie into a glass and garnish with a Fruit Skewer (see page 200), if desired.

Calories	466.94	Protein	7.32 g
Calories from fat	23.84	Total fat	2.65 g
Carbohydrates	112.50 g	Fiber	9.04 g
Calcium	210.16 g	Iron	1.15 mg
Potassium	1168.01 mg	Beta-carotene	3273.49 mcg
Magnesium	90.94 mg	Vitamin C	173.50 mg

Ginseng in the Rain

Even if you haven't inherited a dancing Gene, you'll be twirling your umbrella and tapping your feet with renewed energy after one glassful of this ginseng-enhanced apricot, blueberry, peach, and cherry smoothie.

1 SERVING

½ cup apple juice

1 ½ tablespoons honey

½ cup blueberries

½ cup diced apricots

½ cup diced peach

1 carton (6 ounces) cherry soy yogurt

Ginseng, according to specific-brand label recommendations

Place the apple juice, honey, blueberries, apricots, peach, yogurt, and ginseng in a blender and mix on low speed until the mixture is blended. Continue mixing, gradually increasing the speed, until the mixture is smooth. Pour the smoothie into a glass and garnish with an Apple Chip (see page 192), if desired.

Calories	381.07	Protein	8.37 g
Calories from fat	25.20	Total fat	2.80 g
Carbohydrates	86.43 g	Fiber	5.83 g
Calcium	279.42 g	Iron	2.69 mg
Potassium	640.26 mg	Beta-carotene	1554.38 mcg
Magnesium	20.53 mg	Vitamin C	25.75 mg

How Wheat It Is

This Taylor-made cherry, banana, and strawberry smoothie is one of the most delicious ways to incorporate a healthy portion of wheat germ in your diet. For a novel taste sensation, spoon a generous amount over a bowl of your favorite granola.

1 SERVING

¼ cup orange juice

2 tablespoons vanilla-flavored soy milk

1½ tablespoons honey

½ cup diced cherries

½ cup diced banana

½ cup blackberries

½ cup soft silken tofu

2 tablespoons wheat germ

Place the orange juice, soy milk, honey, cherries, banana, blackberries, tofu, and wheat germ in a blender and mix on low speed until the mixture is blended. Continue mixing, gradually increasing the speed, until the mixture is smooth. Pour the smoothie into a glass and garnish the rim with an Orange Wheel (see page 202), if desired.

Calories	415.72	Protein	12.32 g
Calories from fat	57.71	Total fat	6.41 g
Carbohydrates	84.83 g	Fiber	9.48 g
Calcium	92.82 g	Iron	3.23 mg
Potassium	1105.37 mg	Beta-carotene	177.65 mcg
Magnesium	123.74 mg	Vitamin C	58.18 mg

If I Only Had a Bran

Just keep skipping down the road, and remember, you're off to meet a blizzard in the form of an ice-cold fruit-filled smoothie enhanced with bran, bee pollen, ginkgo, and ginseng. Try it—I guarantee you won't feel "overstuffed."

1 SERVING

5 tablespoons orange juice

3 tablespoons vanilla-flavored soy milk

1 ½ tablespoons honey

1 cup diced banana

½ cup diced mango

½ cup diced strawberries

1 tablespoon wheat bran

1 tablespoon bee pollen

Ginkgo biloba, according to specific-brand label recommendations

Ginseng, according to specific-brand label recommendations

Place the orange juice, soy milk, honey, banana, mango, strawberries, wheat bran, bee pollen, ginkgo, and ginseng in a blender and mix on low speed until the mixture is blended. Continue mixing, gradually increasing the speed, until the mixture is smooth. Pour the smoothie into a glass and garnish with a Fruit Skewer (see page 200), if desired.

Calories	383.52	Protein	4.96 g
Calories from fat	20.67	Total fat	2.30 g
Carbohydrates	95.64 g	Fiber	8.76 g
Calcium	49.33 g	Iron	1.89 mg
Potassium	1122.82 mg	Beta-carotene	2039.83 mcg
Magnesium	97.91 mg	Vitamin C	122.47 mg

It's Not That Peachy Being Green

If you're Kermitted to a healthy lifestyle, you'll find it easy to make a commitment to this delicious green smoothie made with nature's tonic, spirulina.

1 SERVING

¼ cup peach nectar

1½ tablespoons honey

½ cup diced peach

½ cup diced mango

½ cup diced strawberries

1 carton (6 ounces) peach soy yogurt

1 teaspoon spirulina, or according to specific-brand label recommendations

Place the peach nectar, honey, peach, mango, strawberries, yogurt, and spirulina in a blender and mix on low speed until the mixture is blended. Continue mixing, gradually increasing the speed, until the mixture is smooth. Pour the smoothie into a glass and garnish the rim with a Strawberry Fan (see page 215), if desired.

Calories	354.73	Protein	7.75 g
Calories from fat	23.47	Total fat	2.61 g
Carbohydrates	81.05 g	Fiber	5.53 g
Calcium	277.82 g	Iron	2.20 mg
Potassium	475.36 mg	Beta-carotene	2243.28 mcg
Magnesium	24.80 mg	Vitamin C	80.18 mg

Mr. Tea

Listen up! This smoothie is tough. Made with anti-oxidant green tea and a delectable combination of peaches and bananas, it easily defeats the argument that if a smoothie tastes good, it can't be good for you.

1 SERVING

¾ cup vanilla-flavored soy milk

2 green tea bags

¼ cup peach nectar

1 ½ tablespoons honey

1 cup diced peach

½ cup diced banana

½ cup strawberry lowfat frozen yogurt

To make the green-tea ice cubes

Bring ½ cup of the soy milk to a boil in a small saucepan over medium-high heat. Remove the saucepan from the heat and add the tea bags. Allow the tea to steep for 5 to 10 minutes. Squeeze the bags to get as much tea out of them as possible. Pour the tea into a mini ice-cube tray and place in the freezer for several hours or until frozen.

(continues)

To make the smoothie

Remove the green tea cubes from the tray and place them in the blender. Add the remaining ¼ cup soy milk, peach nectar, honey, peach, banana, and yogurt and mix on low speed until the mixture is blended. Continue mixing, gradually increasing the speed, until the mixture is smooth. Pour the smoothie into a glass and garnish with a Pineapple Slice (see page 209), if desired.

Calories	484.70	Protein	11.81 g
Calories from fat	43.01	Total fat	4.78 g
Carbohydrates	105.98 g	Fiber	5.64 g
Calcium	200.96 g	Iron	2.08 mg
Potassium	955.13 mg	Beta-carotene	566.13 mcg
Magnesium	80.94 mg	Vitamin C	22.17 mg

Sammy Soy-Sa

Thump your chest and blow a kiss, because after one sip, you'ill realize that this fruit, soy, and honey smoothie has been very good to you. A perfect refresher for the seventh-inning stretch.

1 SERVING

¼ cup vanilla-flavored soy milk

2 tablespoons orange juice

1½ tablespoons honey

½ cup blueberries

½ cup diced strawberries

½ cup diced banana

1 carton (6 ounces) banana-strawberry soy yogurt

Place the soy milk, orange juice, honey, blueberries, strawberries, banana, and yogurt in a blender and mix on low speed until the mixture is blended. Continue mixing, gradually increasing the speed, until the mixture is smooth. Pour the smoothie into a glass and garnish with Berries on a Skewer (see page 194), if desired.

Calories	391.38	Protein	9.77 g
Calories from fat	35.80	Total fat	3.98 g
Carbohydrates	85.38 g	Fiber	5.79 g
Calcium	284.31 g	Iron	2.74 mg
Potassium	641.78 mg	Beta-carotene	104.48 mcg
Magnesium	47.56 mg	Vitamin C	80.16 mg

Soy Meets Whirl

This smoothie, featuring flavored soy milk and yo-gurt, will be love at first glass.

1 SERVING

½ cup vanilla-flavored soy milk

¼ cup orange juice

1 tablespoon honey

1 cup diced mango

½ cup diced banana

½ cup raspberries

1 carton (6 ounces) raspberry soy yogurt

2 tablespoons granola

1 tablespoon oat bran

Place the soy milk, orange juice, honey, mango, banana, raspberries, yogurt, granola, and oat bran in a blender and mix on low speed until the mixture is blended. Continue mixing, gradually increasing the speed, until the mixture is smooth. Pour the smoothie into a glass and garnish with Berries on a Skewer (see page 194), if desired.

Calories	560.06	Protein	14.59 g
Calories from fat	73.14	Total fat	8.13 g
Carbohydrates	117.57 g	Fiber	10.93 g
Calcium	324.98 g	Iron	4.09 mg
Potassium	990.95 mg	Beta-carotene	3934.15 mcg
Magnesium	101.82 mg	Vitamin C	100.20 mg

Soy to the World

All the boys and girls will fall in love with this tofu, banana, and peanut butter smoothie. If your children are hooked on chocolate peanut butter cups, tempt them with this healthful peanut butter offering instead.

1 SERVING

¼ cup vanilla-flavored Rice Dream

1½ tablespoons honey

1 cup diced banana

½ cup soft silken tofu

3 tablespoons (or more) natural, creamy peanut butter

Place the Rice Dream, honey, banana, tofu, and peanut butter in a blender and mix on low speed until the mixture is blended. Continue mixing, gradually increasing the speed, until the mixture is smooth. Pour the smoothie into a glass and garnish with a Crisp Banana Wafer (see page 198), if desired.

Calories	656.63	Protein	19.41 g
Calories from fat	281.49	Total fat	31.28 g
Carbohydrates	85.38 g	Fiber	7.11 g
Calcium	74.30 g	Iron	2.77 mg
Potassium	1165.77 mg	Beta-carotene	72.00 mcg
Magnesium	153.34 mg	Vitamin C	14.41 mg

Soy, What's New?

Don't ask! But if you really want to know, smoothies made with tofu, soy milk, and lots of fruit are absolutely delicious—and healthful, too.

1 SERVING

½ cup peach nectar

2 tablespoons vanilla-flavored soy milk

1 ½ tablespoons honey

½ cup diced cantaloupe

½ cup diced mango

½ cup diced peach

½ cup soft silken tofu

Place the peach nectar, soy milk, honey, cantaloupe, mango, peach, and tofu in a blender and mix on low speed until the mixture is blended. Continue mixing, gradually increasing the speed, until the mixture is smooth. Pour the smoothie into a glass and garnish with a Fruit Skewer (see page 200), if desired.

Calories	362.84	Protein	8.46 g
Calories from fat	36.92	Total fat	4.10 g
Carbohydrates	79.66 g	Fiber	4.75 g
Calcium	69.51 g	Iron	1.89 mg
Potassium	845.77 mg	Beta-carotene	3844.26 mcg
Magnesium	65.60 mg	Vitamin C	68.98 mg

Spirulina Swirl

Whoever thought these tiny green aquatic plants could be packed with so many healthful benefits? When combined with raspberries and banana, you have one mean green drink.

1 SERVING

2 tablespoons vanilla-flavored soy milk

1½ tablespoons honey

1 cup raspberries

½ cup diced banana

1 carton (6 ounces) raspberry soy yogurt

1 teaspoon spirulina, or according to specific-brand label recommendations

Place the soy milk, honey, raspberries, banana, yogurt, and spirulina in a blender and mix on low speed until the mixture is blended. Continue mixing, gradually increasing the speed, until the mixture is smooth. Pour the smoothie into a glass and garnish with Berries on a Skewer (see page 194), if desired.

Calories	353.75	Protein	8.82 g
Calories from fat	31.66	Total fat	3.52 g
Carbohydrates	77.61 g	Fiber	10.23 g
Calcium	287.07 g	Iron	2.72 mg
Potassium	532.46 mg	Beta-carotene	83.97 mcg
Magnesium	49.44 mg	Vitamin C	38.93 mg

The Flax of Life

Despite what you may have been taught, the stork will not deliver this delicious flax-fortified smoothie to you—you'll have to make it yourself, and you'll be glad you did. The flaxseed oil in this drink elevates your "good" cholesterol and has major health benefits.

1 SERVING

¼ cup vanilla-flavored soy milk

3 tablespoons orange juice

1 ½ tablespoons honey

½ cup blueberries

½ cup diced cherries

½ cup diced strawberries

½ cup soft silken tofu

Flaxseed oil, according to specific-brand label recommendations

Place the soy milk, orange juice, honey, blueberries, cherries, strawberries, tofu, and flaxseed oil in a blender and mix on low speed until the mixture is blended. Continue mixing, gradually increasing the speed, until the mixture is smooth. Pour the smoothie into a glass and garnish the rim with an Orange Wheel (see page 202), if desired.

Calories	334.51	Protein	9.45 g
Calories from fat	48.76	Total fat	5.42 g
Carbohydrates	67.79 g	Fiber	5.80 g
Calcium	78.86 g	Iron	2.32 mg
Potassium	742.30 mg	Beta-carotene	158.27 mcg
Magnesium	68.38mg	Vitamin C	84.97 mg

The Glass Is Always Greener

Forget about searching for a smoothie that is healthier for you than this one. With a healthy dose of nature's tonic—spirulina (it's green)—this smoothie will put a charge in your day.

1 SERVING

¼ cup vanilla-flavored Rice Dream

¼ cup orange juice

1 ½ tablespoons honey

1 cup blueberries

½ cup diced banana

½ cup soft silken tofu

1 teaspoon spirulina, or according to specific-brand label recommendations

Place the Rice Dream, orange juice, honey, blueberries, banana, tofu, and spirulina in a blender and mix on low speed until the mixture is blended. Continue mixing, gradually increasing the speed, until the mixture is smooth. Pour the smoothie into a glass and garnish with Berries on a Skewer (see page 194), if desired.

Calories	412.08	Protein	7.94 g
Calories from fat	63.87	Total fat	7.10 g
Carbohydrates	85.49 g	Fiber	6.52 g
Calcium	67.08 g	Iron	2.03 mg
Potassium	800.70 mg	Beta-carotene	146.06 mcg
Magnesium	69.34 mg	Vitamin C	57.43 mg

The Soy Luck Club

Gather your family around the table and serve them this memorable blueberry, strawberry, and banana smoothie, featuring a healthy portion of soy milk and yogurt as well.

1 SERVING

2 tablespoons vanilla-flavored soy milk

1 ½ tablespoons honey

½ cup blueberries

½ cup diced strawberries

½ cup diced banana

1 carton (6 ounces) blueberry soy yogurt

Place the soy milk, honey, blueberries, strawberries, banana, and yogurt in a blender and mix on low speed until the mixture is blended. Continue mixing, gradually increasing the speed, until the mixture is smooth. Pour the smoothie into a glass and garnish the rim with a Strawberry Fan (see page 215), if desired.

Calories	358.98	Protein	8.69 g
Calories from fat	30.82	Total fat	3.42 g
Carbohydrates	79.45 g	Fiber	5.73 g
Calcium	275.98 g	Iron	2.46 mg
Potassium	547.81 mg	Beta-carotene	92.95 mcg
Magnesium	39.23 mg	Vitamin C	64.66 mg

Tofu Manchu

This inscrutable raspberry, banana, mango, and tofu smoothie is mysteriously delicious! In keeping with the spirit of this smoothie's namesake, serve with fortune cookies.

1 SERVING

½ cup orange juice

1½ tablespoons honey

1 cup raspberries

1 cup diced banana

½ cup diced mango

½ cup soft silken tofu

Place the orange juice, honey, raspberries, banana, mango, and tofu in a blender and mix on low speed until the mixture is blended. Continue mixing, gradually increasing the speed, until the mixture is smooth. Pour the smoothie into a glass and garnish with Berries on a Skewer (see page 194), if desired.

Calories	466.68	Protein	9.49 g
Calories from fat	44.36	Total fat	4.93 g
Carbohydrates	105.77 g	Fiber	13.87 g
Calcium	95.01 g	Iron	2.58 mg
Potassium	1378.31 mg	Beta-carotene	2091.65 mcg
Magnesium	120.23 mg	Vitamin C	129.41 mg

To-fu, or Not To-fu

That is the question. Whether it's nobler to drink one glass of this delightful smoothie or to consume two will be the happy dilemma of most people in your Hamlet.

1 SERVING

¼ cup vanilla-flavored soy milk

¼ cup orange juice

1½ tablespoons honey

1 cup diced peach

1 cup diced banana

½ cup soft silken tofu

Place the soy milk, orange juice, honey, peach, banana, and tofu in a blender and mix on low speed until the mixture is blended. Continue mixing, gradually increasing the speed, until the mixture is smooth. Pour the smoothie into a glass and garnish the rim with an Orange Wheel (see page 202), if desired.

Calories	434.88	Protein	10.43 g
Calories from fat	45.38	Total fat	5.04 g
Carbohydrates	95.35 g	Fiber	7.30 g
Calcium	71.22 g	Iron	2.28 mg
Potassium	1337.50 mg	Beta-carotene	546.75 mcg
Magnesium	105.58 mg	Vitamin C	56.03 mg

Triathlon Turbo

This wheat germ, whey protein, and bee pollen smoothie is the preferred quick energy source for my daughter and favorite triathlete, Laura.

1 SERVING

½ cup vanilla-flavored soy milk

¼ cup orange juice

1½ tablespoons honey

1 cup blueberries

½ cup raspberries

½ cup diced banana

1 tablespoon vanilla-flavored whey protein powder

2 tablespoons wheat germ

1 tablespoon bee pollen, or according to specific-
   brand label recommendations

Place the soy milk, orange juice, honey, blueberries, raspberries, banana, protein powder, wheat germ, and bee pollen in a blender and mix on low speed until the mixture is blended. Continue mixing, gradually increasing the speed, until the mixture is smooth. Pour the smoothie into a glass and garnish with Berries on a Skewer (see page 194), if desired.

Calories	455.58	Protein	13.87 g
Calories from fat	46.13	Total fat	5.13 g
Carbohydrates	97.24 g	Fiber	11.98 g
Calcium	60.74 g	Iron	2.87 mg
Potassium	916.18 mg	Beta-carotene	170.05 mcg
Magnesium	101.56 mg	Vitamin C	72.21 mg

Vit@min CC Rider

Drink this vitamin C—enriched cantaloupe, raspberry, and banana smoothie, and you'll see what you've done to your cold.

1 SERVING

½ cup orange juice

2 tablespoons honey

1 cup diced cantaloupe

½ cup raspberries

½ cup diced banana

½ cup soft silken tofu

1 tablespoon vitamin C, or according to specific-brand label recommendations

Place the orange juice, honey, cantaloupe, raspberries, banana, tofu, and vitamin C in a blender and mix on low speed until the mixture is blended. Continue mixing, gradually increasing the speed, until the mixture is smooth. Pour the smoothie into a glass and garnish the rim with an Orange Wheel (see page 202), if desired.

Calories	402.13	Protein	9.18 g
Calories from fat	40.10	Total fat	4.46 g
Carbohydrates	89.17 g	Fiber	7.71 g
Calcium	86.97 g	Iron	2.27 mg
Potassium	1359.04 mg	Beta-carotene	3178.11 mcg
Magnesium	97.79 mg	Vitamin C	151.93 mg

We're Not in Kansas Anymore, Tofu

This banana, strawberry, and tofu twister will definitely lift you up. Serve it to your friends, and everyone will agree that it's the most Wicked Whip of the Feast.

1 SERVING

¼ cup orange juice

2 tablespoons vanilla-flavored soy milk

1½ tablespoons honey

1 cup diced banana

½ cup diced strawberries

½ cup soft silken tofu

Place the orange juice, soy milk, honey, banana, strawberries, and tofu in a blender and mix on low speed until the mixture is blended. Continue mixing, gradually increasing the speed, until the mixture is smooth. Pour the smoothie into a glass and garnish the rim with a Strawberry Fan (see page 215), if desired.

Calories	368.23	Protein	8.88 g
Calories from fat	42.34	Total fat	4.70 g
Carbohydrates	79.60 g	Fiber	5.81 g
Calcium	69.42 g	Iron	2.19 mg
Potassium	1108.40 mg	Beta-carotene	108.51 mcg
Magnesium	97.06 mg	Vitamin C	91.87 mg

Wheat Are Family

All the brothers and sisters will be singing for more of this delightful kiwi, banana, and wheat germ smoothie.

1 SERVING

¼ cup vanilla-flavored Rice Dream

1½ tablespoons honey

1 cup diced kiwi

½ cup diced banana

1 carton (6 ounces) vanilla soy yogurt

2 tablespoons wheat germ

Place the Rice Dream, honey, kiwi, banana, yogurt, and wheat germ in a blender and mix on low speed until the mixture is blended. Continue mixing, gradually increasing the speed, until the mixture is smooth. Pour the smoothie into a glass and garnish with a Fruit Skewer (see page 200), if desired.

Calories	509.76	Protein	12.14 g
Calories from fat	67.73	Total fat	7.53 g
Carbohydrates	105.95 g	Fiber	10.28 g
Calcium	316.72 g	Iron	3.78 mg
Potassium	1059.39 mg	Beta-carotene	227.16 mcg
Magnesium	109.84 mg	Vitamin C	182.24 mg

Yeast of Eden

There are no tempting apples in this delicious smoothie, but its wonderful combination of cherries, apricots, raspberries, and brewer's yeast makes a highly nutritious treat any Eve.

1 SERVING

⅔ cup apricot nectar

1½ tablespoons honey

½ cup diced apricots

½ cup diced cherries

½ cup raspberries

½ cup raspberry lowfat frozen yogurt

1 tablespoon brewer's yeast, or according to specific-brand label recommendations

Place the apricot nectar, honey, apricots, cherries, raspberries, yogurt, and yeast in a blender and mix on low speed until the mixture is blended. Continue mixing, gradually increasing the speed, until the mixture is smooth. Pour the smoothie into a glass and garnish with Berries on a Skewer (see page 194), if desired.

Calories	413.94	Protein	7.71 g
Calories from fat	25.28	Total fat	2.81 g
Carbohydrates	97.00 g	Fiber	8.90 g
Calcium	203.00 g	Iron	1.92 mg
Potassium	903.90 mg	Beta-carotene	2709.45 mcg
Magnesium	49.30 mg	Vitamin C	30.53 mg

CHAPTER 7

Dazzling Dessert Smoothies

Decadence in a Glass

Smoothies are exciting and versatile offerings that can be enjoyed as a quick snack or incorporated in your diet as a means of reducing calories and fat. But at other times, when you're longing for that occasional indulgence, these glistening glassfuls can easily be transformed into a rich and creamy temptation. When this urge overcomes you, don't even think about the calorie content! Instead, splurge on any of the more than 15 fruit and ice cream sensations found in this chapter—and worry about dieting tomorrow. Made with such rich ingredients as ice cream, chocolate, caramel sauce, and even a few candy bars to tempt you, these smoothies were designed to satisfy your sweet tooth instantly. In fact, these treats are so temptingly delicious that it's hard to believe that a dessert so enriched in vitamins, protein, and calcium could taste so sinfully good.

While this chapter was created for your no-holds-barred indulgence, keep in mind that you can substitute fat-free, lowfat, or reduced-calorie ingredients such as skim milk or fat-free frozen yogurt for ice cream and whole milk if you're watching your calorie and fat consumption. The smoothies won't taste quite as rich as those made with the suggested ingredients, but they will remain flavorful and satisfying.

So, let your hair down and indulge in a creamy glassful of *American Smoothie,* made with raspberry, banana, and blueberry fillings layered into a wine glass, or succumb to *Whirls Just Want to Have Spun,* a delectable combination of peanut butter, banana, chocolate chips, and coconut gelato. You'll find yourself counting the days until the next special occasion.

American Smoothie

*The next time you're having friends over to cele-
brate the Fourth of July or just feeling patriotic,
serve this red, white, and blue smoothie. It's a delicious way to celebrate the Spirit of '76.*

2 SERVINGS

White Smoothie

2 tablespoons milk

¾ cup diced banana

*½ cup Häagen-Dazs Coconut Gelato or favorite
vanilla ice cream*

Red Smoothie

2 tablespoons milk

¾ cup raspberries

*½ cup Häagen-Dazs Coconut Gelato or favorite
vanilla ice cream*

Few drops red food coloring (optional)

Blue Smoothie

2 tablespoons milk

¾ cup blueberries

*½ cup Häagen-Dazs Coconut Gelato or favorite
vanilla ice cream*

Few drops blue food coloring (optional)

To make the white smoothie

Place the milk, banana, and gelato in a blender and mix on low speed until the mixture is blended. Continue mixing, gradually increasing the speed, until the mixture is smooth. Transfer the white smoothie to a bowl and set aside.

To make the red smoothie

Place the milk, raspberries, gelato, and red food coloring (optional) in the blender and mix on low speed until the mixture is blended. Continue mixing, gradually increasing the speed, until the mixture is smooth. Carefully spoon the red smoothie into two wine goblets or glasses, dividing evenly and smoothing the top. Top each with a layer of the white smoothie. Set aside.

To make the blue smoothie

Wipe the blender with a paper towel to remove as much of the red smoothie as possible. Once it's clean, place the milk, blueberries, gelato, and blue food coloring (optional) in the blender and mix on low speed until the mixture is blended. Continue mixing, gradually increasing the speed, until the mixture is smooth. Spoon a layer of the blue smoothie over the white smoothie. Garnish each smoothie with an American flag or raspberries, banana cubes, and blueberries on a skewer, if desired.

Calories	537.89	Protein	10.37 g
Calories from fat	263.33	Total fat	29.26 g
Carbohydrates	59.83 g	Fiber	5.95 g
Calcium	296.23 g	Iron	0.55 mg
Potassium	410.79 mg	Beta-carotene	77.61 mcg
Magnesium	33.46 mg	Vitamin C	24.15 mg

Caramel Miranda

Eat your heart out, Chiquita. You'll have to share center stage with a tempting portion of rich caramel in this scrumptious South American smoothie. This decadent delight is the perfect finale to a casual dinner.

1 SERVING

Caramel Topping

¾ cup granulated sugar

¼ cup cold water

½ teaspoon cream of tartar

½ cup whipping cream

½ teaspoon unsalted butter, at room temperature

Smoothie

3 tablespoons milk

3 tablespoons caramel topping, at room temperature*

1 cup diced banana

2 tablespoons chopped pecans

¾ cup Häagen-Dazs Chocolate Gelato or favorite chocolate ice cream

* Commercially made caramel topping can be substituted for the home-made caramel topping.

To make the caramel topping

Combine the sugar, water, and cream of tartar in a medium-heavy saucepan over medium heat and stir the mixture with a wooden spoon until the sugar dissolves and it comes to a boil. Increase the heat to medium-high and boil, without stirring, for 6 to 8 minutes or until the mixture begins to caramelize and turns a deep amber color, swirling the pan occasionally. Remove the saucepan from the heat. Using a long-handled wooden spoon, add the whipping cream all at once (the mixture will boil vigorously), and stir the mixture until it's well blended. Add the butter and whisk until smooth. Allow the caramel topping to come to room temperature. Transfer the topping to a covered dish and refrigerate until well chilled.

To make the smoothie

Place the milk, caramel topping, banana, pecans, and gelato in a blender and mix on low speed until the mixture is blended. Continue mixing, gradually increasing the speed, until the mixture is smooth. Pour the smoothie into a wine goblet or glass and garnish with a Poppy Seed Caramelized Shard (see page 211), if desired.

Calories	854.51	Protein	12.30 g
Calories from fat	426.59	Total fat	47.40 g
Carbohydrates	100.66 g	Fiber	5.86 g
Calcium	303.39 g	Iron	2.43 mg
Potassium	1137.26 mg	Beta-carotene	x mcg
Magnesium	68.58 mg	Vitamin C	14.48 mg

Ch-apple of Love

Take the plunge and sample the tastes of apples, cinnamon, and caramel ice cream wedded into a perfectly blissful smoothie. Serve this made-in-heaven dessert at your next celebration.

1 SERVING

¼ cup apple juice

1 cup diced apple

¾ cup Häagen-Dazs Dulce de Leche ice cream or
   favorite vanilla ice cream

¼ teaspoon ground cinnamon

Place the apple juice, apple, ice cream, and cinnamon in a blender and pulse to blend on low speed until the mixture is blended. Continue mixing, gradually increasing the speed, until the mixture is smooth. Pour the smoothie into a wine goblet or glass and garnish with two Cinnamon-Coated Fusilli (see page 195), if desired.

Calories	509.59	Protein	7.80 g
Calories from fat	247.68	Total fat	27.52 g
Carbohydrates	58.20 g	Fiber	3.72 g
Calcium	243.22 g	Iron	0.50 mg
Potassium	217.53 mg	Beta-carotene	26.83 mcg
Magnesium	8.11 mg	Vitamin C	7.69 mg

Daddy Starbucks

Like its namesake, this heavenly combination of coffee, fudge, banana, and caramel ice cream is extremely rich; but go ahead and splurge—the sun will come up tomorrow. Serve this ambrosial delight "Annie" time you're having friends over for a backyard barbecue.

1 SERVING

Hot Fudge Sauce

2 tablespoons whipping cream

2 tablespoons light corn syrup

1 tablespoon canola oil

4 ounces semisweet chocolate, chopped

2 tablespoons milk

Smoothie

1/2 cup prepared coffee, well chilled

2 tablespoons hot fudge sauce, at room temperature*

1 cup diced banana

3/4 cup Häagen-Dazs Dulce de Leche ice cream or favorite vanilla ice cream

* Commercially made hot fudge sauce can be substituted for the home-made hot fudge sauce.

To make the hot fudge sauce

Combine 1 tablespoon whipping cream, corn syrup, and oil in a small, heavy saucepan over medium-high heat and bring to a boil, stirring occasionally. Remove the saucepan from the heat and add the chocolate; blend well. Add the milk and 1 tablespoon whipping cream and whisk until well blended. Allow the mixture to cool for 10 minutes. Transfer the hot fudge sauce to a covered container and refrigerate.

To make the smoothie

Place the coffee, fudge sauce, banana, and ice cream in a blender and mix on low speed until the mixture is blended. Continue mixing, gradually increasing the speed, until the mixture is smooth. Pour the smoothie into a wine goblet or glass and garnish with an Almond Triangle (see page 190), if desired.

Calories	707.88	Protein	10.31 g
Calories from fat	346.67	Total fat	38.52 g
Carbohydrates	86.03 g	Fiber	4.80 g
Calcium	253.12 g	Iron	1.17 mg
Potassium	745.05 mg	Beta-carotene	72.00 mcg
Magnesium	74.13 mg	Vitamin C	13.73 mg

Espresso Express

Head for the kitchen, nonstop. You'll be immensely pleased with the strikingly rich coffee flavor of this absolutely delicious smoothie. Garnish it with a Spritz Cookie (see page 213), which also makes a tasty edible spoon.

1 SERVING

½ cup espresso, well chilled

1 cup diced banana

¾ cup vanilla ice cream

Place the espresso, banana, and ice cream in a blender and pulse to blend on low speed until the mixture is smooth. Pour the smoothie into a wine goblet or glass.

Calories	553.80	Protein	9.06 g
Calories from fat	251.42	Total fat	27.94 g
Carbohydrates	68.48 g	Fiber	3.60 g
Calcium	236.40 g	Iron	0.62 mg
Potassium	732.00 mg	Beta-carotene	72.00 mcg
Magnesium	139.50 mg	Vitamin C	13.89 mg

Good Golly, Miss Maui

This pineapple and coconut Hawaiian delight is a Little Richer, but it's definitely worth the splurge. For a special presentation, remove the top of a small pineapple and scoop out the fruit inside. Serve this paradisiacal delight in the pineapple shell.

1 SERVING

⅓ cup pineapple juice

1 cup diced pineapple

½ cup diced banana

¾ cup Häagen-Dazs Coconut Gelato or favorite vanilla ice cream

Place the pineapple juice, pineapple, banana, and gelato in a blender and mix on low speed until the mixture is blended. Continue mixing, gradually increasing the speed, until the mixture is smooth. Pour the smoothie into a wine goblet or glass and garnish with a Lemon Pirouette (see page 203), if desired.

Calories	593.28	Protein	8.88 g
Calories from fat	252.24	Total fat	28.03 g
Carbohydrates	78.28 g	Fiber	3.66 g
Calcium	240.35 g	Iron	0.81 mg
Potassium	575.48 mg	Beta-carotene	85.13 mcg
Magnesium	43.45 mg	Vitamin C	50.70 mg

Heath Wave

When the temperature outside is rising, this Heath Wave will cool you down. Made with Heath bars, caramel, and ice cream, it's ideal party fare for the young or young at heart and will satisfy the candy lover in you.

1 SERVING

2 tablespoons milk

1 cup diced banana

2 tablespoons caramel topping, at room temperature (see page 146)*

1 package (1.4 ounces) Heath milk-chocolate English toffee bar, broken into small pieces

¾ cup Häagen-Dazs Dulce de Leche ice cream or favorite vanilla ice cream

Place the milk, banana, caramel topping, Heath bar, and ice cream in a blender and mix on low speed until the mixture is blended. Continue mixing, gradually increasing the speed, until the mixture is smooth. Pour the smoothie into a wine goblet or glass and garnish with an Almond Triangle (see page 190), if desired.

* Commercially made caramel topping can be substituted for the home-made caramel topping.

Calories	898.69	Protein	13.00 g
Calories from fat	428.92	Total fat	47.66 g
Carbohydrates	110.96 g	Fiber	3.60 g
Calcium	280.29 g	Iron	0.50 mg
Potassium	682.50 mg	Beta-carotene	72.00 mcg
Magnesium	48.70 mg	Vitamin C	14.03 mg

La Bamba Banana

Bamba la Bamba, Bamba la Bamba, Bamba la Bamba, Bamba la Bamba Ba! Or, loosely translated, this creamy banana smoothie makes an impressive finale to a south-of-the-border dinner party.

1 SERVING

1 tablespoon butter

½ tablespoon firmly packed dark-brown sugar

3 tablespoons orange juice

1 cup diced banana (unfrozen)

¾ cup vanilla ice cream

Melt the butter in a small saucepan over medium heat. Add the brown sugar and cook, stirring constantly, until the mixture caramelizes. Add the orange juice and blend well. Add the banana and stir-fry for 1 minute. Remove the pan from the heat and cool for 10 minutes. Cover the pan and refrigerate for several hours or until well chilled. Place the chilled banana mixture and ice cream in a blender and mix on low speed until the mixture is smooth. Pour the smoothie into a wine goblet or glass and garnish with a Crisp Banana Wafer (see page 198), if desired.

Calories	691.50	Protein	9.49 g
Calories from fat	353.88	Total fat	39.32 g
Carbohydrates	78.18 g	Fiber	3.69 g
Calcium	248.36 g	Iron	0.71 mg
Potassium	714.48 mg	Beta-carotene	89.30 mcg
Magnesium	50.89 mg	Vitamin C	36.90 mg

Little Bo-Peach

Don't lose the recipe for this smoothie, or you'll never be able to baaaa-sk in the delight of its rich peach and raspberry flavors. For an impressive presentation, starting at the top, carefully scoop the pit and some of the fruit (leave about a 1/4-inch-thick wall) out of a whole, firm peach and then fill the cavity with this delightful mixture.

1 SERVING

¼ cup cold water

2 tablespoons granulated sugar

½ teaspoon vanilla extract

1 ½ cups diced peach

¾ cup Häagen-Dazs Raspberry Gelato or favorite
 ice cream

To make the syrup

Place the water, sugar, and vanilla in a small saucepan over medium-high heat and bring to a boil. Simmer for 3 minutes. Allow the syrup to cool for 10 minutes. Cover the saucepan and refrigerate for several hours or until well chilled.

(continues)

To make the smoothie

Place the syrup, peach, and gelato in a blender and mix on low speed until the mixture is blended. Continue mixing, gradually increasing the speed, until the mixture is smooth. Pour the smoothie into a wine goblet or glass and garnish with a Lemon Pirouette (see page 203), if desired.

Calories	617.64	Protein	9.29 g
Calories from fat	245.08	Total fat	27.23 g
Carbohydrates	85.05 g	Fiber	5.10 g
Calcium	239.42 g	Iron	0.30 mg
Potassium	506.06 mg	Beta-carotene	677.53 mcg
Magnesium	18.70 mg	Vitamin C	16.83 mg

Mason-Dixon Lime

Rhett and Scarlett would have approved of this Southern delight. Serve this refreshing treat as a snack or light dessert at your next family gathering.

1 SERVING

3 tablespoons fresh lime juice

1 cup diced banana

¾ cup Häagen-Dazs Coconut Gelato or favorite vanilla ice cream

Place the lime juice, banana, and gelato in a blender and blend on low speed until the mixture is blended. Continue mixing, gradually increasing the speed, until the mixture is smooth. Pour the smoothie into a wine goblet or glass and garnish with a Lemon Pirouette (see page 203), if desired.

Calories	555.45	Protein	9.25 g
Calories from fat	249.90	Total fat	27.77 g
Carbohydrates	70.80 g	Fiber	3.78 g
Calcium	238.15 g	Iron	0.48 mg
Potassium	644.28 mg	Beta-carotene	74.54 mcg
Magnesium	46.27 mg	Vitamin C	27.16 mg

Mocha-Motion

When you're suffering from the midday blahs, grab a glass of this rich chocolate smoothie and do the mocha-motion with glee. This spectacular blend, designed to satisfy your sweet tooth, can be served as a sensuous finale after a light dinner.

1 SERVING

2 tablespoons milk

2 tablespoons hot fudge sauce, at room temperature (see page 149)*

I cup diced banana

¾ cup Häagen-Dazs Cappuccino Gelato or favorite coffee ice cream

2 tablespoons toasted hazelnuts, chopped**

Place the milk, hot fudge sauce, banana, gelato, and hazelnuts in a blender and mix on low speed until the mixture is blended. Continue mixing, gradually increasing the speed, until the mixture is smooth. Pour the smoothie into a wine goblet or glass and garnish with a Walnut Meringue Shard (see page 216), if desired.

* Commercially made hot fudge sauce can be substituted for the home-made hot fudge sauce.

** To toast the hazelnuts: Place them in a shallow pan and bake at 350 degrees F (in a preheated oven) for 10 to 15 minutes or until fragrant.

Calories	814.51	Protein	13.34 g
Calories from fat	434.40	Total fat	48.27 g
Carbohydrates	89.38 g	Fiber	6.20 g
Calcium	303.43 g	Iron	1.80 mg
Potassium	825.17 mg	Beta-carotene	75.45 mcg
Magnesium	95.72 mg	Vitamin C	14.93 mg

My Cherry Amour

It's no "Wonder" that everyone with a sweet tooth falls in love with this creamy and intensely fla-vored smoothie made from cherries, banana, and ice cream. Serve this delight as a perfect finale to a rich meal or enjoy it as an afternoon splurge.

1 SERVING

⅓ cup apple juice

1 tablespoon honey

1 cup diced cherries

½ cup diced banana

¾ cup vanilla ice cream

Place the apple juice, honey, cherries, banana, and ice cream in a blender and mix on low speed until the mixture is smooth. Pour the smoothie into a wine goblet or glass and garnish with a Walnut Meringue Shard (see page 216), if desired.

Calories	681.66	Protein	10.13 g
Calories from fat	259.59	Total fat	28.84 g
Carbohydrates	100.18 g	Fiber	5.26 g
Calcium	258.31 g	Iron	1.19 mg
Potassium	731.19 mg	Beta-carotene	204.39 mcg
Magnesium	40.60 mg	Vitamin C	17.82 mg

Pinball Blizzard

Watch the flavor points rack up when you treat yourself to this malted–milk-ball smoothie blended with bananas and ice cream. It's a sure replay. Score even more points by sharing this candy delight winner with friends.

1 SERVING

3 tablespoons milk

1 cup diced banana

¾ cup vanilla ice cream

½ cup (or more) malted–milk-balls, coarsely chopped

Place the milk, banana, and ice cream in a blender and mix on low speed until the mixture is smooth. Add the malted balls and pulse to blend. Pour the smoothie into a wine goblet or glass and garnish with a Spritz Cookie (see page 213), if desired.

Calories	1133.55	Protein	17.69 g
Calories from fat	533.69	Total fat	59.30 g
Carbohydrates	140.67 g	Fiber	6.55 g
Calcium	482.36 g	Iron	1.34 mg
Potassium	1052.50 mg	Beta-carotene	72.00 mcg
Magnesium	105.20 mg	Vitamin C	14.42 mg

Razzle Dazzle Raspberry Cheesecake

No smoke and mirrors are needed. If you're looking for a way to impress your friends, surprise them by serving up a glassful of this raspberry cheesecake smoothie for dessert. They will be bedazzled. To complete the cheesecake experience, top this decadent delight with a thin layer of crushed graham crackers.

1 SERVING

2 tablespoons milk

¼ teaspoon vanilla extract

1 cup raspberries

2 ounces cream cheese, at room temperature

¾ cup Häagen-Dazs Raspberry Gelato or favorite ice cream

Place the milk, vanilla, raspberries, cream cheese, and gelato in a blender and mix on low speed until the mixture is blended. Continue mixing, gradually increasing the speed, until the mixture is smooth. Pour the smoothie into a wine goblet or glass and garnish with a Lemon Pirouette (see page 203), if desired.

Calories	685.00	Protein	13.90 g
Calories from fat	436.20	Total fat	48.47 g
Carbohydrates	48.80 g	Fiber	8.36 g
Calcium	333.83 g	Iron	1.40 mg
Potassium	302.40 mg	Beta-carotene	47.97 mcg
Magnesium	29.76 mg	Vitamin C	31.04 mg

The Gre@t Pumpkin Smoothie

You can stop waiting for the Great Pumpkin to appear—it's here in the form of this deliciously rich smoothie. Best of all, you can make it for Peanuts. But don't wait for Halloween to serve this offering; it can be enjoyed any time of the year.

1 SERVING

1 tablespoon milk

½ cup solid-packed pumpkin, chilled

½ cup diced banana

1½ tablespoons firmly packed dark-brown sugar

¼ teaspoon ground cinnamon

¾ cup vanilla ice cream

Place the milk, pumpkin, banana, brown sugar, cinnamon, and ice cream in a blender and blend on low speed until the mixture is smooth. Pour the smoothie into a wine goblet or glass and garnish with a Cinnamon-Coated Tortilla Triangle (see page 197), if desired.

Calories	604.26	Protein	10.15 g
Calories from fat	253.92	Total fat	28.21 g
Carbohydrates	80.14 g	Fiber	5.63 g
Calcium	302.15 g	Iron	2.38 mg
Potassium	643.89 mg	Beta-carotene	15991.48 mcg
Magnesium	57.95 mg	Vitamin C	12.12 mg

Whirls Just Want to Have Spun

Cyndi knows how to have a good time, and you can, too! Serve this richly flavored chocolate chip, peanut butter, and coconut gelato smoothie as a midday indulgence or tempting dessert.

1 SERVING

2 tablespoons milk

1 cup diced banana

2 tablespoons natural, creamy peanut butter

2 tablespoons chocolate chips

¾ cup Häagen-Dazs Coconut Gelato or favorite vanilla ice cream

Place the milk, banana, peanut butter, chocolate chips, and gelato in a blender and blend on low speed until the mixture is blended. Continue mixing, gradually increasing the speed, until the mixture is smooth. Pour the smoothie into a wine goblet or glass and garnish with a Spritz Cookie (see page 213), if desired.

Calories	855.07	Protein	19.02 g
Calories from fat	464.00	Total fat	51.56 g
Carbohydrates	87.88 g	Fiber	6.76 g
Calcium	289.38 g	Iron	1.75 mg
Potassium	933.37 mg	Beta-carotene	72.00 mcg
Magnesium	123.34 mg	Vitamin C	13.94 mg

You da Mango

Next time you're having friends over for a barbe-cue, serve this funky glass of mango sweetness and watch the high fives appear.

1 SERVING

3 tablespoons milk

1 cup diced mango

¾ cup Häagen-Dazs Coconut Gelato or favorite vanilla ice cream

Place the milk, mango, and gelato in a blender and mix on low speed until the mixture is blended. Continue mixing, gradually increasing the speed, until the mixture is smooth. Pour the smoothie into a wine goblet or glass and garnish with a Lemon Pirouette (see page 203), if desired.

Calories	540.34	Protein	9.85 g
Calories from fat	260.76	Total fat	28.97 g
Carbohydrates	61.68 g	Fiber	2.97 g
Calcium	295.94 g	Iron	0.24 mg
Potassium	326.94 mg	Beta-carotene	3851.10 mcg
Magnesium	20.98 mg	Vitamin C	46.14 mg

CHAPTER 8

Cocktail Hour

Perfect Party Smoothies

Imagine being invited to a dinner party, and in place of a traditional mixed drink or after-dinner cocktail, your host offers you a cocktail *smoothie* instead. It's true—the simple addition of liqueur or spirits to some of your favorite smoothie ingredients can result in an uptown temptation that reaches a dimension in elegance and distinction never dreamed of before. Equally exciting, when a cocktail smoothie is served in a champagne flute or wine goblet, it will make your guests forget that they ever preferred a Bailey's or a martini. But the union of spirits and smoothies doesn't end here. With the addition of ice cream, a tempting cocktail can easily be transformed into an elegant dessert. When these mealtime showstoppers are garnished with a Cinnamon-Coated Tortilla Triangle (see page

197) or a Lemon Pirouette (see page 203), everyone at your table will agree—move over chocolate mousse.

As you glance at the recipes in this chapter created for company-quality smoothies, you'll see familiar ones named for their traditional cocktail counterparts, such as *Brandy Alexander* and *Black Russian,* while others, such as *Summer Freeze* or *Magnolia Blossom,* may not be as well known to you. What distinguishes them all, however, is that their ingredients meld well with a dash of spirits, resulting in a refreshing glassful with a pleasing bite.

So gather your swizzle sticks and miniature paper umbrellas and you'll soon agree that these smoothies have earned their place among the rich and famous.

Banana Daiquiri

Daiquiri is a small town on the east coast of Cuba. It's believed that the daiquiri was created by iron mine workers who used to enjoy this drink after a long day's work. Satisfy your thirsty guests with a refreshing glassful of this richly flavored banana daiquiri, which can be enjoyed before or after dinner.

1 SERVING

1 ½ tablespoons light rum

1 ½ tablespoons crème de banana or other banana liqueur

1 ½ tablespoons white crème de cacao

1 teaspoon fresh lime juice (optional)

1 cup diced banana

1 cup vanilla ice cream

Place the rum, banana liqueur, crème de cacao, lime juice (optional), banana, and ice cream in a blender and mix on low speed until the mixture is blended. Continue mixing, gradually increasing the speed, until the mixture is smooth. Pour the smoothie into a wine goblet or glass and garnish with an Almond Triangle (see page 190), if desired.

Calories	870.85	Protein	12.15 g
Calories from fat	361.10	Total fat	40.12 g
Carbohydrates	90.99 g	Fiber	3.60 g
Calcium	312.51 g	Iron	0.53 mg
Potassium	604.41 mg	Beta-carotene	72.00 mcg
Magnesium	44.24 mg	Vitamin C	13.65 mg

Bananarama

*To appreciate the full extent of this banana fla-
vored smoothie, serve it in a champagne flute and
garnish it with a Spritz Cookie (see page 213). It's
the ideal dessert to serve after a casual dinner.*

1 SERVING

2 tablespoons light rum

1 tablespoon crème de banana or other banana
    liqueur

1 tablespoon blue curacao

1 cup diced banana

1 cup vanilla ice cream

Place the rum, banana liqueur, curacao, banana,
and ice cream in a blender and mix on low speed
until the mixture is blended. Continue mixing,
gradually increasing the speed, until the mixture
is smooth.

Calories	794.74	Protein	11.94 g
Calories from fat	350.51	Total fat	38.95 g
Carbohydrates	84.36 g	Fiber	3.60 g
Calcium	311.27 g	Iron	0.50 mg
Potassium	598.81 mg	Beta-carotene	72.00 mcg
Magnesium	43.78 mg	Vitamin C	13.65 mg

Black Russian

One of Mother Russia's greatest contributions to mankind is vodka. Without it, we would never be able to enjoy the ever-popular Black Russian cocktail. When traditional ingredients of Kahlúa and vodka are combined with banana and ice cream, the end result is a delicious concoction that can be served as a special aperitif or sensuous dessert.

1 SERVING

3 tablespoons vodka

2 tablespoons Kahlúa or other coffee liqueur

I cup diced banana

I cup vanilla ice cream

Place the vodka, Kahlúa, banana, and ice cream in a blender and mix on low speed until the mixture is blended. Continue mixing, gradually increasing the speed, until the mixture is smooth. Pour the smoothie into a wine goblet or glass and garnish with a Spritz Cookie (see page 213), if desired.

To make a White Russian, use the same ingredients in the above recipe except add 3 tablespoons coffee liqueur.

Calories	874.54	Protein	11.56 g
Calories from fat	331.25	Total fat	36.81 g
Carbohydrates	89.68 g	Fiber	3.60 g
Calcium	309.14 g	Iron	0.49 mg
Potassium	598.67 mg	Beta-carotene	72.00 mcg
Magnesium	43.93 mg	Vitamin C	13.65 mg

Brandy Alexander

Brandy is distilled from fruit, such as apples, blackberries, grapes, and apricots. When Brandy Alexander ingredients are combined with banana and ice cream, you create the ultimate smoothie dessert to enjoy after a light meal. It's especially impressive when this delectable concoction is served in a brandy balloon glass and complemented with a plateful of assorted of dainty butter cookies.

1 SERVING

1 tablespoon brandy

1 tablespoon white crème de cacao

¾ cup diced banana

¾ cup vanilla ice cream

Place the brandy, crème de cacao, banana, and ice cream in a blender and mix on low speed until the mixture is blended. Continue mixing, gradually increasing the speed, until the mixture is smooth. Pour the smoothie into a brandy balloon glass or wine goblet and garnish with two Cinnamon-Coated Fusilli (see page 195), if desired.

Calories	590.72	Protein	8.67 g
Calories from fat	248.24	Total fat	27.58 g
Carbohydrates	64.12 g	Fiber	2.70 g
Calcium	231.82 g	Iron	0.36 mg
Potassium	447.90 mg	Beta-carotene	54.00 mcg
Magnesium	32.84 mg	Vitamin C	10.24 mg

California Dreaming

This apricot and brandy-laced smoothie is named after the golden state of California. One glassful of this golden-colored delight will start you dreaming about the next time you can indulge in it. Serve this as a refreshing offering at a brunch or as a light dessert.

1 SERVING

3 tablespoons brandy

2 tablespoons orange juice

1 cup diced apricots

1 cup orange sorbet

Place the brandy, orange juice, apricots, and sorbet in a blender and mix on low speed until the mixture is blended. Continue mixing, gradually increasing the speed, until the mixture is smooth. Pour the smoothie into a wine goblet or glass and garnish the rim with an Orange Wheel (see page 202), if desired.

Calories	470.21	Protein	2.53 g
Calories from fat	6.35	Total fat	0.71 g
Carbohydrates	93.57 g	Fiber	4.02 g
Calcium	26.51 g	Iron	0.97 mg
Potassium	711.23 mg	Beta-carotene	2580.58 mcg
Magnesium	16.61 mg	Vitamin C	72.75 mg

Cosmopolitan

The Cosmopolitan is probably the most widely known of the new-age cocktail classics. If you want to impress your friends, surprise them with a martini glass full of this sophisticated orange, cranberry, and vodka-flavored smoothie.

1 SERVING

¼ cup vodka

1 tablespoon cranberry juice

½ tablespoon cointreau

1 cup diced orange

¾ cup orange sorbet

Place the vodka, cranberry juice, cointreau, orange, and sorbet in a blender and mix on low speed until the mixture is blended. Continue mixing, gradually increasing the speed, until the mixture is smooth. Pour the smoothie into a wine goblet or glass and garnish the rim with an Orange Wheel (see page 202), if desired.

Calories	448.95	Protein	1.70 g
Calories from fat	1.67	Total fat	0.19 g
Carbohydrates	78.59 g	Fiber	3.98 g
Calcium	66.51 g	Iron	0.23 mg
Potassium	418.16 mg	Beta-carotene	55.65 mcg
Magnesium	16.92 mg	Vitamin C	130.70 mg

Danish Snowball

If you adore the flavor of cherries in a dessert, "Denmark" my word, this cherry-flavored smoothie, enriched with a classic Danish cherry liqueur, will make an impressive finale to any meal.

1 SERVING

2 tablespoons Cherry Heering liqueur or other cherry liqueur

1 cup diced cherries

1 cup vanilla ice cream

Place the Cherry Heering liqueur, cherries, and ice cream in a blender and mix on low speed until the mixture is blended. Continue mixing, gradually increasing the speed, until the mixture is smooth. Pour the smoothie into a wine goblet or glass and garnish with a Poppy Seed Caramelized Shard (see page 211), if desired.

Calories	716.69	Protein	11.85 g
Calories from fat	336.53	Total fat	37.39 g
Carbohydrates	75.24 g	Fiber	3.33 g
Calcium	322.03 g	Iron	0.59 mg
Potassium	329.05 mg	Beta-carotene	168.06 mcg
Magnesium	15.95 mg	Vitamin C	10.15 mg

Dejà Blueberry

Serve this delightfully, light dessert after a casual meal and be prepared to provide seconds. Your guests will definitely want to sample Dejà Blueberry all over again.

1 SERVING

2 tablespoons Grand Marnier or other orange liqueur

1 cup blueberries

¾ cup ice cream

Place the Grand Marnier, blueberries, and ice cream in a blender and blend on low speed until the mixture is blended. Continue mixing, gradually increasing the speed, until the mixture is smooth. Pour the smoothie into a wine goblet or glass and garnish with a Lemon Pirouette (see page 203), if desired.

Calories	586.42	Protein	8.49 g
Calories from fat	248.72	Total fat	27.64 g
Carbohydrates	64.52 g	Fiber	3.92 g
Calcium	233.84 g	Iron	0.26 mg
Potassium	133.30 mg	Beta-carotene	87.00 mcg
Magnesium	7.68 mg	Vitamin C	18.85 mg

Kahlúa Hummer

Combining Kahlúa, banana, and ice cream is the ultimate taste experience. This sensational smoothie can be served as a light dessert or an aperitif.

1 SERVING

2 tablespoons Kahlúa or other coffee liqueur

1 tablespoon light rum

¾ cup diced banana

1 cup vanilla ice cream

Place the Kahlúa, rum, banana, and ice cream in a blender and mix on low speed until the mixture is blended. Continue mixing, gradually increasing the speed, until the mixture is smooth. Pour the smoothie into a wine goblet or glass and garnish with a Cinnamon-Coated Tortilla Triangle (see page 197), if desired.

Calories	775.83	Protein	11.17 g
Calories from fat	329.63	Total fat	36.63 g
Carbohydrates	80.89 g	Fiber	2.70 g
Calcium	306.89 g	Iron	0.38 mg
Potassium	450.03 mg	Beta-carotene	54.00 mcg
Magnesium	33.05 mg	Vitamin C	10.24 mg

Magnolia Blossom

Aside from warm hospitality, all you need to complement this Southern delight is a group of good friends enjoying a candlelight dinner on your deck. Be sure to have some good bourbon so that you can appropriately flavor this mealtime sweet finale. Miniature pecan and lemon tarts make the perfect dessert accompaniment.

1 SERVING

2 tablespoons milk

2 tablespoons bourbon

¼ teaspoon vanilla extract

1 cup diced banana

¾ cup vanilla ice cream

Place the milk, bourbon, vanilla, banana, and ice cream in a blender and mix on low speed until the mixture is blended. Continue mixing, gradually increasing the speed, until the mixture is smooth. Pour the smoothie into a wine goblet or glass and garnish with a Crisp Banana Wafer (see page 198), if desired.

Calories	629.07	Protein	10.05 g
Calories from fat	258.65	Total fat	28.74 g
Carbohydrates	68.20 g	Fiber	3.60 g
Calcium	270.41 g	Iron	0.49 mg
Potassium	642.52 mg	Beta-carotene	72.00 mcg
Magnesium	47.72 mg	Vitamin C	13.94 mg

Mango Margarita

There are a number of stories floating around about the origin of the margarita. A widely believed one is that a socialite named Margarita Sames of San Antonio, Texas, created the drink for poolside sipping at her Christmas party in Acapulco in 1948. However, Carlos Herrera claims to have made the first margarita in 1938 at Rancho La Gloria, located south of Tijuana, for a showgirl who could only drink tequila. Other stories abound, but you can create your own legend by sharing this sensational mango and tequila smoothie with good friends at your next fiesta.

1 SERVING

2 tablespoons tequila

1 tablespoon triple sec

1 tablespoon Grand Marnier or other orange liqueur

1 cup diced mango

¾ cup orange sorbet

(continues)

Place the tequila, triple sec, Grand Marnier, mango, and sorbet in a blender and mix on low speed until the mixture is blended. Continue mixing, gradually increasing the speed, until the mixture is smooth. Pour the smoothie into a wine goblet or glass and garnish the rim with a Lime Wheel (see page 202), if desired.

Calories	482.24	Protein	0.86 g
Calories from fat	4.77	Total fat	0.53 g
Carbohydrates	94.58 g	Fiber	2.97 g
Calcium	16.64 g	Iron	0.24 mg
Potassium	382.21 mg	Beta-carotene	3851.10 mcg
Magnesium	15.28 mg	Vitamin C	76.27 mg

Mimosa

This orange and champagne smoothie is ideal fare to serve at a brunch. It's also a refreshing indulgence in when lounging around the pool.

1 SERVING

½ cup good-quality champagne

1 ½ cups diced orange

½ cup orange sorbet

Place the champagne, orange, and sorbet in a blender and mix on low speed until the mixture is blended. Continue mixing, gradually increasing the speed, until the mixture is smooth. Pour the smoothie into a wine goblet or glass and garnish the rim with an Orange Wheel (see page 202), if desired.

Calories	333.61	Protein	2.74 g
Calories from fat	2.00	Total fat	0.22 g
Carbohydrates	67.62 g	Fiber	5.94 g
Calcium	99.00 g	Iron	0.30 mg
Potassium	520.55 mg	Beta-carotene	82.91 mcg
Magnesium	24.75 mg	Vitamin C	162.19 mg

Mudslide Madness

*There's no end to the number of ways you can cre-
ate a mudslide. I like to keep the ingredients simple
so that each flavor can be savored.*

1 SERVING

1 to 1½ tablespoons Kahlúa or other coffee
    liqueur

1 to 1½ tablespoons Baileys Original Irish Cream
    or other Irish cream liqueur

1 to 1½ tablespoons vodka

¾ cup diced banana

1 cup vanilla ice cream

Place the Kahlúa, Baileys, vodka, banana, and ice
cream in a blender and mix on low speed until
the mixture is blended. Continue mixing, gradually increasing the speed, until the mixture is
smooth. Pour the smoothie into a wine goblet or
glass and garnish with a Poppy Seed Caramelized
Shard (see page 211), if desired.

Calories	772.07	Protein	11.56 g
Calories from fat	349.27	Total fat	38.81 g
Carbohydrates	77.59 g	Fiber	2.70 g
Calcium	309.09 g	Iron	0.38 mg
Potassium	425.30 mg	Beta-carotene	54.00 mcg
Magnesium	33.12 mg	Vitamin C	10.24 mg

Peach Bellini

This smoothie says amore! Serve this peach and champagne delight when peaches are at their ripest, then wait for the pinches.

1 SERVING

¼ cup good-quality champagne

2 tablespoons vodka

2 tablespoons peach schnapps

1 cup diced peach

¾ cup orange sorbet

Place the champagne, vodka, peach schnapps, peach, and sorbet in a blender and mix on low speed until the mixture is blended. Continue mixing, gradually increasing the speed, until the mixture is smooth. Pour the smoothie into a wine goblet or glass and garnish the rim with an Orange Wheel (see page 202), if desired.

Calories	453.05	Protein	1.28 g
Calories from fat	1.38	Total fat	0.15 g
Carbohydrates	74.28 g	Fiber	3.40 g
Calcium	8.50 g	Iron	0.19 mg
Potassium	455.46 mg	Beta-carotene	451.69 mcg
Magnesium	11.90 mg	Vitamin C	41.78 mg

Piña Colada

In the 1950s, a Puerto Rican named Don Ramón Lopez-Irizarry created coconut cream, which was made from the tender white part of the coconut. A few years later, a bartender came up with the idea to mix rum and pineapple juice with coconut cream, and the Piña Colada, one of Puerto Rico's favorite drinks, was born. One taste of this Piña Colada smoothie, and it's certain to become a favorite of yours, too.

1 SERVING

¼ cup light rum

1 cup diced pineapple

1 cup Häagen-Dazs Coconut Gelato or favorite vanilla ice cream

Place the rum, pineapple, and gelato in a blender and mix on low speed until the mixture is blended. Continue mixing, gradually increasing the speed, until the mixture is smooth. Pour the smoothie into a wine goblet or glass and garnish with a Pineapple Chip (see page 207), if desired.

Calories	744.39	Protein	10.60 g
Calories from fat	330.00	Total fat	36.67 g
Carbohydrates	61.20 g	Fiber	1.86 g
Calcium	310.85 g	Iron	0.64 mg
Potassium	176.26 mg	Beta-carotene	18.13 mcg
Magnesium	21.70 mg	Vitamin C	23.87 mg

Sangria

If you've never tasted a sangria smoothie, you're in for a pleasant surprise. This wine and fruit delight is ideally suited for deckside dining, especially when enjoying Spanish fare. Top it off with a garnish of apple and orange wedges for an authentic touch.

2 SERVINGS

2 tablespoons granulated sugar

2 tablespoons cold water

½ cup chilled red wine

1 tablespoon brandy

2 teaspoons triple sec

1 cup diced apple

1 cup diced orange

2 cups orange sorbet

To make simple syrup

Place the sugar in a small glass and add boiling water. Stir until the sugar dissolves. Cover the glass and refrigerate until well chilled.

(continues)

To make the smoothie

Place the syrup, wine, brandy, triple sec, apple, orange, and sorbet in a blender and mix on low speed until the mixture is blended. Continue mixing, gradually increasing the speed, until the mixture is smooth. Pour the smoothie into two wine goblets or glasses and garnish with apple and orange wedges, if desired.

Calories	479.01	Protein	1.09 g
Calories from fat	2.82	Total fat	0.31 g
Carbohydrates	106.68 g	Fiber	3.67 g
Calcium	42.54 g	Iron	0.48 mg
Potassium	445.89 mg	Beta-carotene	40.39 mcg
Magnesium	19.26 mg	Vitamin C	91.59 mg

Strawberry Daiquiri

This tangy yet sweet tequila and strawberry blend is appropriate to serve as a cocktail before dinner or as a light dessert to enjoy after a filling meal.

1 SERVING

3 tablespoons tequila

1 ½ tablespoons triple sec

1 teaspoon fresh lime juice (optional)

1 cup diced strawberries

¾ cup strawberry sorbet

Place the tequila, triple sec, lime juice (optional), strawberries, and sorbet in a blender and mix on low speed until the mixture is blended. Continue mixing, gradually increasing the speed, until the mixture is smooth. Pour the smoothie into a wine goblet or glass and garnish the rim with a Strawberry Fan (see page 215), if desired.

Calories	417.67	Protein	1.05 g
Calories from fat	6.15	Total fat	0.68 g
Carbohydrates	69.51 g	Fiber	5.34 g
Calcium	23.81 g	Iron	0.66 mg
Potassium	285.17 mg	Beta-carotene	27.17 mcg
Magnesium	17.23 mg	Vitamin C	113.62 mg

Summer Freeze

This remarkably refreshing smoothie, made with a combination of tropical ingredients, is an ideal libation to enjoy when relaxing on your deck or lounging around the pool.

1 SERVING

2 tablespoons dark rum

1 tablespoon triple sec

1 tablespoon pineapple juice

1 cup diced orange

¾ cup Häagen-Dazs Coconut Gelato or favorite vanilla ice cream

Place the rum, triple sec, pineapple juice, orange, and gelato in a blender and mix on low speed until the mixture is blended. Continue mixing, gradually increasing the speed, until the mixture is smooth. Pour the smoothie into a wine goblet or glass and garnish with a Pineapple Wedge (see page 209), if desired.

Calories	603.35	Protein	9.21 g
Calories from fat	244.72	Total fat	27.19 g
Carbohydrates	58.83 g	Fiber	3.96 g
Calcium	291.07 g	Iron	0.24 mg
Potassium	315.76 mg	Beta-carotene	61.09 mcg
Magnesium	16.71 mg	Vitamin C	98.29 mg

The Berry Thought of You

The intriguing combination of blackberries, crème de cassis, and ice cream in this smoothie is definitely memorable. For added enjoyment, serve this creamy dessert with a plateful of miniature berry tarts.

1 SERVING

3 tablespoons milk

1 tablespoon crème de cassis

1 cup blackberries

¾ cup vanilla ice cream

Place the milk, crème de cassis, blackberries, and ice cream in a blender and mix on low speed until the mixture is blended. Continue mixing, gradually increasing the speed, until the mixture is smooth. Pour the smoothie into a wine goblet or glass and garnish with a Walnut Meringue Shard (see page 216), if desired.

Calories	560.56	Protein	10.04 g
Calories from fat	262.19	Total fat	29.13 g
Carbohydrates	57.90 g	Fiber	7.63 g
Calcium	325.52 g	Iron	0.85 mg
Potassium	351.78 mg	Beta-carotene	69.12 mcg
Magnesium	34.93 mg	Vitamin C	30.67 mg

CHAPTER 9

Glorious Garnishes

A Touch of Class

Smoothies are usually known for their unique combination of flavors and textures rather than for their appearance. Yet for many special occasions, a well-chosen garnish can magically create a visually grand presentation out of this simple combination of fruit and other ingredients. A basic fruit smoothie can be artfully embellished with a *Pineapple Bow* or an *Orange Wheel*. And, when hosting an important dinner party, you can easily elevate a smoothie dessert to a memorable experience by presenting it in an attractive wine goblet and garnishing it with a *Cinnamon-Coated Tortilla Triangle* or a *Pineapple Chip*. What's more, each of these garnishes is, in itself, exceptionally delicious.

In this chapter, you'll find a host of novel ideas for creating garnishes that dress up a smoothie. Most of the garnishes found in this chapter are not difficult to make, and you may choose to make them well in advance and keep several frozen so you can have a ready supply of these delights for an instant smoothie celebration. On the other hand, if you don't have the time or inclination to make your own garnishes, consider picking up some fun accessories at your neighborhood party store, such as multicolored and uniquely shaped straws, cocktail umbrellas, brightly colored metallic sparklers, or fancy swizzle sticks. Also, a number of edible accessories are available on the Internet, such as Cookie Straws, which are chocolate lined and vanilla or strawberry flavored, and Cookie Spoons, made of edible cookies that can be purchased plain or chocolate dipped. You can order these fantastic treats online at www.gicco.com.

While it's true that most smoothies are so inherently appealing that they're not really in need of embellishment, I'm convinced that once you've seen the effect an artfully garnished smoothie has on your family or guests, you'll agree that this added touch is just like framing a Renoir.

Almond Triangles

These quick and easy almond triangles look terrific as a garnish when inserted upright into any of the smoothies made with dairy products or alcohol. Another kudo for these crunchy delights is that they taste great, too.

16 TO 20 TRIANGLES

Nonstick cooking spray

¼ cup (½ stick) unsalted butter, cut into small pieces

¼ cup granulated sugar

1 tablespoon whipping cream

1 tablespoon light corn syrup

¾ cup sliced almonds

¼ cup rolled oats

Preheat oven to 375 degrees F. Line a baking sheet with parchment paper. Lightly coat the paper with a nonstick vegetable spray. Combine the butter, sugar, whipping cream, and corn syrup in a medium saucepan over medium-high heat. Bring to a boil, stirring occasionally. Reduce the heat to medium and add the almonds and oats; blend well. Cook for 3 minutes, stirring constantly. Using a metal spatula, spread the almond mixture onto the prepared baking sheet and form into an 8- by 6-inch rectangle (it does not have to be exact). Bake for 8 to 9 minutes or until the almond mixture begins to spread and turns brown. Remove the baking sheet from the oven and place it on a cooling rack. When cool, place another baking sheet over the baked almond triangle, and invert the baking sheet. Cut into triangles (or break into irregular shapes). Store the almond triangles in an airtight container for two to three days.

Calories	80.44	Protein	1.38 g
Calories from fat	50.73	Total fat	5.64 g
Carbohydrates	6.58 g	Fiber	0.71 g
Calcium	14.83 g	Iron	0.12 mg
Potassium	39.20 mg	Beta-carotene	0 mcg
Magnesium	17.74 mg	Vitamin C	0.01 mg

Apple Chips

Apple Chips are crunchy, paper-thin slices of apples. They are the perfect garnish to dress up any smoothie. Not only do they add a sophisticated elegance to smoothies or other desserts, but they are delicious as well. The chips are best when the apples are thinly sliced with a mandolin or vegetable slicer; however, with a little patience, a sharp knife can be just as effective.

16 TO 20 CHIPS

1 Granny Smith or Golden Delicious apple, unpeeled and uncored

4 cups cold water

1/4 cup fresh lemon juice

2 cups granulated sugar

Preheat oven to 200 degrees F. Line a baking sheet with parchment paper or a silicone baking mat. Set aside. Thinly slice the apples into horizontal rings, about 1/16-inch thick. Place the apple rings in a bowl filled with 2 cups water and 2 tablespoons lemon juice. Set aside. Combine the remaining 2 cups water and 2 tablespoons lemon juice and sugar in a large saucepan over medium-high heat and cook for 3 to 4 minutes or until the mixture comes to a boil, stirring frequently to dissolve the sugar. Add the apples and cook for 1 to 2 minutes or until the mixture returns to a boil. Transfer the apples to a sieve placed over a bowl; drain well. Place the apples in a single layer on the prepared baking sheet. Pat the apple rings with a double layer of paper towels. Bake for 1 hour or until the apple rings are dry. If the apple rings are not dry after an hour, turn off the oven and allow them to dry in the oven. The apple chips can be stored in an airtight container for up to three days.

Calories	28.46	Protein	0.03 g
Calories from fat	0	Total fat	0 g
Carbohydrates	7.48 g	Fiber	0.17 g
Calcium	0.63 g	Iron	0.02 mg
Potassium	11.98 mg	Beta-carotene	0.27 mcg
Magnesium	0.46 mg	Vitamin C	1.31 mg

Berries on a Skewer

This beautiful yet easy-to-prepare garnish adds a rich color to most smoothies.

2 SKEWERS

½ cup fresh raspberries, blueberries, blackberries, or cranberries

2 wooden skewers, 6 to 10 inches long

Thread five to six berries of your choice onto the upper half of each skewer.

Calories	15.07	Protein	0.28 g
Calories from fat	1.52	Total fat	0.17 g
Carbohydrates	3.56 g	Fiber	2.09 g
Calcium	6.76 g	Iron	0.18 mg
Potassium	46.74 mg	Beta-carotene	11.99 mcg
Magnesium	5.54 mg	Vitamin C	7.69 mg

Cinnamon-Coated Fusilli

This garnish provides a delightful way to add a whimsical touch to a special smoothie, ice cream sundae, or almost any dessert.

8 FUSILLI

2 tablespoons granulated sugar

1 teaspoon ground cinnamon

4 to 8 gourmet fusilli pasta

Canola oil for frying

Line a baking sheet with a double layer of paper towels. Set aside. Combine the sugar and cinnamon in a small bowl and blend well. If the pasta is U shaped, break each one into two equal pieces. Each piece should be about 9 inches in length. Pour enough oil in a 10-inch skillet about 1 inch deep. Place the skillet over medium-high heat for at least 2 minutes or until the oil registers 350 degrees F. Place four pieces of pasta in the oil and fry for about 1 to 2 minutes or just until they begin to brown. (The fusilli will continue to brown after they are

(continues)

removed from the oil.) Using tongs, transfer the fusilli to the prepared pan and immediately sprinkle with sugar and cinnamon mixture. Repeat this process with the remaining fusilli. Store the cinnamon-coated fusilli in an airtight container.

Calories	19.23	Protein	0.27 g
Calories from fat	5.58	Total fat	0.62 g
Carbohydrates	3.22 g	Fiber	0.13 g
Calcium	2.15 g	Iron	0.14 mg
Potassium	4.09 mg	Beta-carotene	0.22 mcg
Magnesium	1.07 mg	Vitamin C	0.04 mg

Cinnamon-Coated Tortilla Triangles

These triangles are so delicious that you might want to make extra. They are fabulous as a garnish when inserted upright into a smoothie.

8 TO 12 TRIANGLES

2 tablespoons unsalted butter, melted

1 tablespoon firmly packed dark-brown sugar

¼ teaspoon ground cinnamon

1 8-inch flour tortilla

Preheat oven to 350 degrees F. Line a baking sheet with parchment paper. Set aside. Melt the butter in a small saucepan over medium-low heat. Add the brown sugar and cinnamon and blend well. Using a pastry brush, brush the tortilla with the butter mixture. Place the tortilla on the prepared baking sheet. Cut the tortilla into eight to twelve triangles and bake for 10 minutes or until crisp. Store the cinnamon-coated tortilla triangles in an airtight container.

Calories	52.01	Protein	0.57 g
Calories from fat	29.81	Total fat	3.31 g
Carbohydrates	5.13 g	Fiber	0.24 g
Calcium	5.34 g	Iron	0.25 mg
Potassium	14.89 mg	Beta-carotene	0.14 mcg
Magnesium	2.16 mg	Vitamin C	0.00 mg

Crisp Banana Wafers

These crispy wafers are simply made of pureed bananas and sugar that have been baked in a slow oven until the mixture becomes brown and crisp. When cool, it is broken into irregular pieces that can be used to adorn any of the smoothies found in this book.

12 TO 16 WAFERS

2 medium bananas, cut into 1-inch pieces

1 to 2 tablespoons granulated sugar

Preheat the oven to 200 degrees F. Line a baking sheet with a silicone baking mat. Set aside. Place the bananas and sugar in the work bowl of a food processor fitted with a metal blade (or in a blender) and process for 45 seconds or until the bananas are pureed. Spoon the pureed bananas onto the center of the prepared baking sheet. Using a metal spatula, spread the puree evenly into a rectangular shape, about $\frac{1}{16}$-inch thick. The layer should almost cover the mat. Bake the banana puree for $2\frac{1}{2}$ to 3 hours or until brown and completely dry. Remove the pan from the oven, place another baking sheet over the baked banana, and invert the pan. Gently remove the silicone pad and allow the baked banana to cool for 30 minutes to an hour. When cool, break into irregular triangular shapes. The crisp banana wafers can be stored in an airtight container for up to three days.

Calories	24.03	Protein	0.17 g
Calories from fat	1.50	Total fat	0.17 g
Carbohydrates	6.37 g	Fiber	0.50 g
Calcium	0.01 g	Iron	0.06 mg
Potassium	0.02 mg	Beta-carotene	0 mcg
Magnesium	0 mg	Vitamin C	1.50 mg

Fruit Skewers

Fruit Skewers make an attractive smoothie garnish when inserted into a tall glass. What's more, the fruit is a delicious complement to the smoothie. The combination and arrangement of fruits chosen from the list below is almost infinite. Also, keep in mind that even a skewer containing a single fruit, such as melon balls, can be as lovely as one made with a variety.

2 SKEWERS

2 grapes

2 kiwi slices, peeled and cut 1-inch thick

2 banana slices, peeled and cut 1-inch thick

2 pineapple cubes

2 melon balls

2 strawberries

2 stemless maraschino cherries

2 star fruit, cut ½-inch thick

2 wooden skewers, 6 to 10 inches long

Alternately thread different fruit onto the upper half of the skewers, ending with the strawberry on the top. Be sure to use skewers that are long enough to allow the bottom piece of fruit to rest comfortably on the rim of the glass. The fruit skewers can be kept refrigerated in an airtight container for up to 2 hours. (If using bananas, toss the slices in a little lemon juice to prevent them from turning brown.)

Calories	43.87	Protein	0.52 g
Calories from fat	1.88	Total fat	0.21 g
Carbohydrates	11.51 g	Fiber	1.42 g
Calcium	7.90 g	Iron	0.24 mg
Potassium	134.21 mg	Beta-carotene	293.64 mcg
Magnesium	8.60 mg	Vitamin C	27.39 mg

Lemon, Lime, and Orange Wheels

If you're fortunate enough to have a garnishing set that includes a food decorator tool or canalling knife, follow the instructions given. If these tools are unavailable, you'll find that this technique for making fruit wheels, taught to me by my mother, is quite simple and requires only a fork.

5 TO 6 WHEELS

1 lemon, lime, or orange

Using a fork, start at one end of the fruit and move the fork down to the other end, slightly piercing the skin. Repeat this process around the entire fruit. Remove the ends and cut the fruit into ¼-inch-thick slices. To hang the wheel over the rim of a glass, make a slit by cutting through the peel and halfway into the flesh. Fit the slit over the rim of the glass.

Calories	x	Protein	x g
Calories from fat	x	Total fat	x g
Carbohydrates	x g	Fiber	x g
Calcium	x g	Iron	x mg
Potassium	x mg	Beta-carotene	x mcg
Magnesium	x mg	Vitamin C	x mg

Lemon Pirouettes

Garnishing with one of these cookies is a delicious way to adorn many smoothies. Although there are a host of commercially made pirouettes that come in assorted sizes and flavors, I prefer to make my own. If lemon is not your favorite flavor, simply omit the lemon peel and substitute 2 tablespoons of honey for the lemon juice.

12 PIROUETTES

4 tablespoons unsalted butter, at room temperature

2 tablespoons fresh lemon juice

½ cup powdered sugar

½ cup flour

1 teaspoon finely grated lemon peel

1 large egg white, beaten until foamy

Preheat oven to 375 degrees F. Line a baking sheet with parchment paper or a silicone mat (or use a nonstick baking sheet). Set aside. Place the butter and lemon juice in a medium bowl and beat with a handheld electric mixer on medium speed for 1 minute or until well combined. Add

(continues)

the powdered sugar, flour, and lemon peel and beat on low speed for 2 to 3 minutes or until smooth and creamy, scraping down the sides of the bowl with a rubber spatula as necessary. Add the egg white and beat just until incorporated. Spoon 1 rounded tablespoon batter onto each half of the prepared baking sheet. Spread the batter with the back of a spoon into a 5-inch circle. (Don't worry if the batter looks uneven—it will even out during the baking process.) Bake for 7 to 10 minutes or until the edges begin to turn golden brown. Allow the cookies to cool for 1 minute, then lift each with a metal spatula to loosen it and quickly roll up the cookie into a tight cylinder or cigar shape. Place the cookies, seam side down, on a cake rack to cool completely. Repeat the process with the remaining batter. The cookies can be stored in an airtight container for up to three to five days or frozen for a couple of weeks.

Calories	72.13	Protein	0.85 g
Calories from fat	34.57	Total fat	3.84 g
Carbohydrates	8.75 g	Fiber	0.15 g
Calcium	1.75 g	Iron	0.25 mg
Potassium	8.73 mg	Beta-carotene	0.35 mcg
Magnesium	0.58 mg	Vitamin C	1.38 mg

Mint Leaves

Mint Leaves make an attractive accent when used to garnish a smoothie. The trick is to keep the leaves crisp.

1 bunch mint leaves

Remove any rubber bands first. Next, cut off the root ends and lower part of the stems because they draw moisture from the fragile leaves. Once trimmed, loosely wrap the mint in a damp paper towel and place it in a large enough plastic bag so that the leaves and stems will not be crushed. Place the mint on the top shelf of your refrigerator and use it within a few days. If the mint needs washing before use, simply immerse it in a bowl filled with cold water and swish it around with your hands. Scoop it up and gently blot dry with a paper towel or put it in a salad spinner.

Calories	0.04	Protein	0.00 g
Calories from fat	0.00	Total fat	0.00 g
Carbohydrates	0.01 g	Fiber	0.00 g
Calcium	0.12 g	Iron	0.00 mg
Potassium	0.28 mg	Beta-carotene	1.28 mcg
Magnesium	0.04 mg	Vitamin C	0.02 mg

Pineapple Bow

Smoothies go uptown when garnished with this colorful and tasty pineapple bow tie.

4 BOWS

1 pineapple, bottom and spiny leaves and core removed

4 stemless maraschino cherries

4 wooden skewers, 10 inches long

Slice the pineapple (with its rind) into ½-inch-thick slices. Cut the slices into eight triangular segments, each about 1½ inches wide at the bottom and 1½ inches high from the bottom to top. (The remaining pineapple can be cut into cubes and placed in the freezer to be made into a smoothie.) Thread one pineapple segment, rind side down, onto the upper half of a skewer. Thread a cherry on the skewer so that its rests on the point of the pineapple segment. Thread another pineapple segment, point side down, so that the tip rests on the cherry. Push the fruit to the top of the skewer, but be sure that the skewer is not poking out of the top pineapple segment. Store the pineapple bows in an airtight container for up to 2 hours.

Calories	16.86	Protein	0.05 g
Calories from fat	0.54	Total fat	0.06 g
Carbohydrates	4.73 g	Fiber	0.17 g
Calcium	0.98 g	Iron	0.05 mg
Potassium	15.82 mg	Beta-carotene	1.64 mcg
Magnesium	1.96 mg	Vitamin C	2.16 mg

Pineapple Chips

This garnish can elevate pineapple smoothies, and many others, to a new dimension. The chips are deliciously sweet and look sensational when inserted upright into a smoothie. This is also a perfect garnish for a dish of sorbet or ice cream.

12 TO 18 CHIPS

1 fresh pineapple, top, bottom, sides, and core removed

1 cup granulated sugar

1 cup cold water

Preheat oven to 225 degrees F. Line a baking sheet with a silicone mat. Set aside. Using a mandolin or vegetable slicer, if possible, thinly slice the pineapple into horizontal rings, about ⅟₁₆-inch thick. With patience, the pineapple rings can be sliced with a knife. Place the pineapple rings in a shallow roasting pan. Set aside. Combine the sugar and water together in a small, heavy saucepan over moderate heat and bring to a boil, stirring occasionally. Pour the hot mixture over the pineapple rings and cover the pan with aluminum foil. Place the pan over two stove burners; cook over low heat for 15 minutes.

(continues)

Remove the pan from the burners, allowing the pineapple rings to cool to room temperature. Once the pineapple rings are cool, place them on the prepared baking sheet and bake for 60 to 90 minutes or until they turn golden brown. As soon as the pineapple chips are baked, they can be kept whole, formed into a rolled cigar shape, or cut into wedges. Allow the pineapple chips to cool before storing them in an airtight container for up to two days. The pineapple chips will become crisp as they cool.

Note: The pineapple chips can also be made by thinly slicing the pineapple into rings and placing them on a double thickness of paper towels. Pat the tops of each pineapple ring with paper towels, then transfer them to a baking sheet lined with a silicone mat. Sprinkle ¼ teaspoon granulated sugar over each pineapple ring and bake in a preheated oven at 350 degrees F for 60 to 90 minutes or until golden brown.

Calories	35.40	Protein	0.15 g
Calories from fat	1.52	Total fat	0.17 g
Carbohydrates	9.04 g	Fiber	0.47 g
Calcium	2.79 g	Iron	0.15 mg
Potassium	44.53 mg	Beta-carotene	4.60 mcg
Magnesium	5.51 mg	Vitamin C	6.06 mg

Pineapple Spears, Wedges, and Slices

Pineapple Spears, Wedges, or Slices perched on the rim of a glass add a tasty, tropical flair to a smoothie. To get the sweetest part of the pineapple, use the section closest to the top, near the spiny leaves. Consider leaving the outside rind on the pineapple for added color.

4 SPEARS, WEDGES, OR SLICES

1 small pineapple

To make the pineapple spears, cut the pineapple in half, lengthwise. Cut one half of the pineapple into quarters and make an incision parallel with the core. Place the pineapple spear on the rim of the glass. (The remaining pineapple can be cut into cubes and placed in the freezer to be made into a smoothie.) To make the pineapple wedges, place the pineapple on its side and cut into ½-inch-thick slices; cut each slice in half. Cut each half into wedges, about 3 inches wide at the bottom and 2½ inches high from the bottom to top. Make a slit by cutting through the

(continues)

rind and halfway into the pineapple wedge. Fit the slit over the rim of the glass. To make the pineapple slices, place the pineapple on its side and cut into ½-inch-thick slices; cut each slice in half. Make a slit by cutting through the rind and halfway into the pineapple. Fit the slit over the rim of the glass.

Calories	27.44	Protein	0.22 g
Calories from fat	2.17	Total fat	0.24 g
Carbohydrates	6.94 g	Fiber	0.67 g
Calcium	3.92 g	Iron	0.21 mg
Potassium	63.28 mg	Beta-carotene	6.55 mcg
Magnesium	7.84 mg	Vitamin C	8.62 mg

Poppy Seed Caramelized Shards

This versatile garnish adds a whimsical touch to most smoothies. They can be shaped into almost any design you desire and are amazingly easy to make. Each shard can also be dipped in melted chocolate for an even more dramatic presentation. If you prefer not to add poppy seeds, simply omit them from the recipe.

12 TO 16 SHARDS

½ cup granulated sugar

2 tablespoons cold water

½ tablespoon poppy seeds

Line a baking sheet with parchment paper. Set aside. Combine the sugar and water in a small, heavy saucepan over moderate heat. Bring the mixture to a boil, stirring frequently with a wooden spoon to dissolve the sugar. Add the poppy seeds and blend well. Continue boiling, without stirring, for 6 to 7 minutes or until the mixture turns amber or pale golden in color, swirling the pan occasionally. Remove the saucepan from the heat. Slowly pour the caramel

(continues)

mixture in a free-form pattern onto the prepared baking sheet. Allow it to cool. When cool, break the caramelized mixture into irregular triangular shapes. The poppy seed caramelized shards can be stored in an airtight container for up to three days.

Calories	34.12	Protein	0.06 g
Calories from fat	1.41	Total fat	0.16 g
Carbohydrates	8.41 g	Fiber	0.04 g
Calcium	5.20 g	Iron	0.04 mg
Potassium	2.62 mg	Beta-carotene	0 mcg
Magnesium	1.18 mg	Vitamin C	0.01 mg

Spritz Cookies

These richly flavored cookies add just the right amount of sweetness to many of the dessert smoothies. I like to use them straight from the freezer so they remain firm when inserted upright in a smoothie.

4 TO 5 DOZEN COOKIES

1 cup (2 sticks) unsalted butter, at room temperature

1 cup powdered sugar

1 large egg

1 teaspoon vanilla extract

2⅓ cups flour

¼ teaspoon coarse salt

Preheat the oven to 400 degrees F. Line two baking sheets with parchment paper. Set aside. In the mixing bowl of an electric mixer (or with a handheld beater), beat the butter on medium-high speed until creamy. Gradually add the sugar and beat until well combined. Add the egg and vanilla and blend well, scraping down the sides of the bowl with a rubber spatula as necessary.

(continues)

Reduce the speed to low and add the flour and salt and beat until just combined. Spoon the batter into a large pastry bag fitted with a French or open-star tip (½ inch in diameter). Pipe the batter onto the prepared baking sheets into 5- to 6-inch fingers, 1 inch apart. (Or use a heaping teaspoonful for each cookie and roll between your hands into a 5 to 6-inch cigar shape.) Bake for 7 to 10 minutes or until the cookies are light brown around the edges. Remove the pan from the oven and place it on a cooling rack. When cool, store the cookies in an airtight container. Serve at room temperature, chilled, or frozen.

Calories	64.89	Protein	0.75 g
Calories from fat	35.48	Total fat	3.94 g
Carbohydrates	6.60 g	Fiber	0.15 g
Calcium	1.68 g	Iron	0.30 mg
Potassium	2.67 mg	Beta-carotene	0 mcg
Magnesium	0.21 mg	Vitamin C	0 mg

Strawberry Fans

Strawberry Fans add a nice touch of color when placed on the rim of a glass and are a tasty treat as well.

2 FANS

2 whole, firm strawberries, unhulled

Using a very sharp knife, make vertical cuts through the strawberry, starting from just below the top and cutting through to the bottom. Make about five to six very thin cuts, depending on the size of the strawberry. Place the strawberry on a plate and carefully spread the slices apart to resemble an opened fan. Slip a strawberry fan over the rim of each glass.

Calories	5.63	Protein	0.13 g
Calories from fat	0	Total fat	0 g
Carbohydrates	1.50 g	Fiber	0.50 g
Calcium	2.50 g	Iron	0.09 mg
Potassium	-- mg	Beta-carotene	0 mcg
Magnesium	-- mg	Vitamin C	12.00 mg

Walnut Meringue Shards

These nutty garnishes are easy to make and add a delicious crunchy flavor when eaten with a smoothie.

12 TO 16 SHARDS

1 large egg white

2 tablespoons granulated sugar

½ cup finely chopped walnuts

Preheat oven to 350 degrees F. Line a baking sheet with parchment paper. Place the egg white and sugar in a small mixing bowl and beat with a handheld beater on medium speed until foamy. Add the walnuts and blend well. Spread the mixture onto the prepared baking sheet into a 9- by 7-inch rectangle (it does not have to be exact) and bake for 15 to 20 minutes or until brown. Cool completely. Break the meringue into pieces or cut into triangles. Store in an airtight container for up to four days.

Calories	41.07	Protein	1.56 g
Calories from fat	26.52	Total fat	2.95 g
Carbohydrates	2.74 g	Fiber	0.26 g
Calcium	3.21 g	Iron	0.16 mg
Potassium	31.31 mg	Beta-carotene	9.38 mcg
Magnesium	10.83 mg	Vitamin C	0.17 mg

Index